Revised Edition

KNOWLEDGE WHIZZ 4

Kunal Savarkar Seema Chari

Collins

KNOWLEDGE WHIZZ 4

Revised Edition

Kunal Savarkar • Seema Chari

Student + Teacher			Teacher-only	
a animations	**ia** activities	**g** games	**lp** lesson plans	**tn** teacher's notes
ilt instructor-led tutorials	**w** worksheets	**v** videos	**w** worksheets	**ak** answer keys
	audio			

Preface

Welcome to ***Knowledge Whizz*** Version 2.0! Our belief that knowledge is for everyone has resonated well across the country, with thousands of school children now using the series, thereby reinforcing our conviction that general knowledge is not the exclusive preserve of a few quizzers. In this multimedia age, knowledge is everywhere, but sourcing, assimilating and recalling it is a skill that can be learned!

Knowledge Whizz, now in its second edition, is a unique series that aims to offer general knowledge covering a wide range of subjects, both curricular as well as extra-curricular, to children from six to thirteen years of age. These are GK books for learning, not quiz books for testing.

Salient features of the series

- Each task comprises at least two kinds of inputs to help children arrive at the answers and acquire knowledge at the same time.
- Tasks cover a wide range of topics presented with a twist. For instance, history includes the story of the automobile, bicycle, cinema, cricket and flight; science includes accidental inventions and discoveries; geography comes alive through associative information and culturally rich chapters. Language and literature cover trivia and etymology, two wonderful learning tools.
- Themes from modern life such as gaming, media, business and finance are extensively explored as well as tidbits about the quirky and the quotidian.
- **India-specific content** presented beautifully through fun, richly illustrated tasks, designed to whet the curiosity of children and inspire them to explore their beautiful country in all its diversity. New chapters on **North East India** bring the vibrancy and uniqueness of this relatively lesser known part of India to children everywhere.
- The books do not expect children to be pre-equipped with knowledge but instead reward inquisitiveness by giving them workoutable tasks.
- The artistic and colourful layouts make the presentation more accessible, exciting and alluring whilst facilitating self-learning.
- Special features are an exciting mixed bag of environment education, life skills, values, quick quizzes, cool facts, cool activity, evaluation of multiple intelligences and Higher Order Thinking Skills to make children become well-rounded individuals.
- Brand new features incorporated into Version 2.0 include **Aptitudes**, aiming to hone and cement specific verbal, visual and logical aptitudes through the common lens of general knowledge, **Safety Science**, which draws our attention to the science behind the measures we should take to stay safe wherever we are, and **Game**, to bring a good dose of fun into learning.

We gratefully acknowledge the contribution of the Xpress Minds Edutainment team, whose inputs have been invaluable for this second edition.

We are certain that this series will open up the world of general knowledge and make learning a fun, instinctive and rewarding process for all.

~ Kunal Savarkar and Seema Chari

In This Book ...

Travelling to a Hill Station

A. *These are some signs you will see when you travel in the hills. Do you know what they mean? Write the meaning of each sign inside the box next to it. Take help from the icons, which will give you the clues. The first one is done for you.*

Multiple Intelligence tasks focus on the 8 Intelligences: interpersonal, intrapersonal, bodily kinesthetic, visual-spatial, logical reasoning, verbal-linguistic, naturalistic and musical. Each page explores 5-6 intelligences to encourage learners to learn in their own way and is not to be used for assessment.

Higher Order Thinking Skills (HOTS) pages encourage critical thinking and teach learners to analyse and evaluate information. Cool quizmaster, Kunal Savarkar, helps students become knowledge detectives and skilled quizzers.

How to Crack the Indian State Capitals

To learn and remember the names of capitals of 29 states and 7 union territories of India is not very easy.

Cool Activity
Fun activities to learn through doing.

Cool Quiz
Encourages research to find solutions.

Current Affairs
Visit **www.collins.in/knowledgewhizz** for Current Affairs updates and weekly quizzes.

Sporting Spirit

All sports teach us ethics, fair play and the
all of us both on and off the playing field.
We should remember and follow these values

Match these sentences about the right way to
play a sport and write the correct number-letter

Values pages focus on inculcating values, morals, ethics and right attitudes in students through to-do tasks.

Aptitude

Aptitude Tasks are designed to teach children to develop specific skills such as sequencing, classification, analogies and others through rebuses, matching, sorting and pattern activities, with step-by-step tips on how to solve them.

Life Skills pages expose learners to problems in real-life situations to help them learn to take decisions.

Visit to a Fuel static

Have you been to a fuel station?

A. *Look at the picture and label*
parts. But watch out! There a
wrong labels.

COOL FACT

The bicycle is the mode of transport of the common man. It consumes no fuel, it is healthy and cheap– in short, a great combination.

Green Earth

Green Earth page focuses on environmental issues and imbibes the right attitude towards conservation of environment.

COOL FACT

Factoids linked to the content of the page. The fun element in them will make you say, 'Hey! Cool to know that.'

Safety Science

Safety is not just a notion; it is a science, which means it is guided by research, facts and figures. From home to school, public places to controlled environments, we can do a lot to keep ourselves safe. The Safety Science chapters in each book show us how.

Game

Life is a game! Each book in the series has at least one puzzle, maze or strategy-based activity, always with a GK twist, but with the added feel-good incentive of "winning the game".

Quiz Yourself are quick quizzes to assess what the children have learned in the book. The main themes and the cool facts will all form the basis of the Quiz Yourself section, intended as a self-evaluation tool from books 3 to 8.

Detailed Contents

Contents

Flowers

Flowers are beautiful. They are also useful in many ways. Flowers give us oil, spices, dyes and perfumes. Some flowers can even be eaten.

Look at the flowers below and match them with their uses.

1. 
sunflower

2. 
jasmine

3. 
broccoli

4. 
rose

5. 
clove

6. 
saffron

7. 
marigold

8. 
banana

9. 
hibiscus

a. spice, medicinal oil

b. edible

c. edible

d. edible, perfumes and fragrance, hair ornaments

e. edible oil, yellow dye

f. red food colouring, beverage

g. perfume, fragrance, hair ornaments

h. garlands

i. flavouring, yellow dye

COOL FACT

Some flowers actually emit a rotting-flesh smell. Rafflesia, the biggest flower in the world, is an example. It is also called a 'carrion flower'.

ART

2 Mixing Colours

Red, blue and yellow are primary colours. You can make many different colours by mixing them.

A. *Given below are overlapping circles of different colours. Combine the two original colours to fill in the overlapped space with the correct colour. Use water or poster paints to mix the colours on a palette with a brush and see what colour you get.*

1.
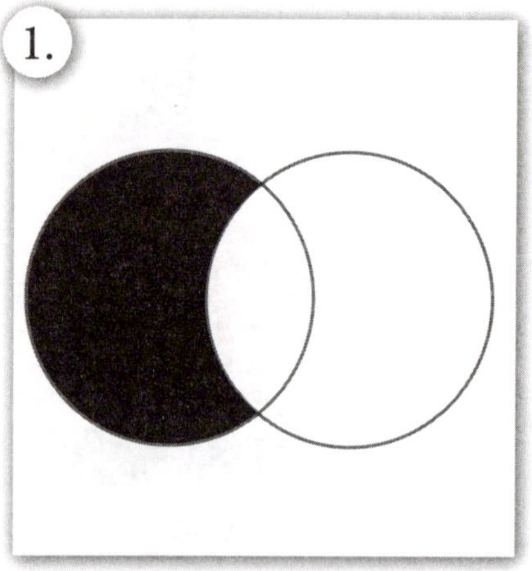

black-white

2.

yellow-blue

3.

blue-red

4.

red-white

5.
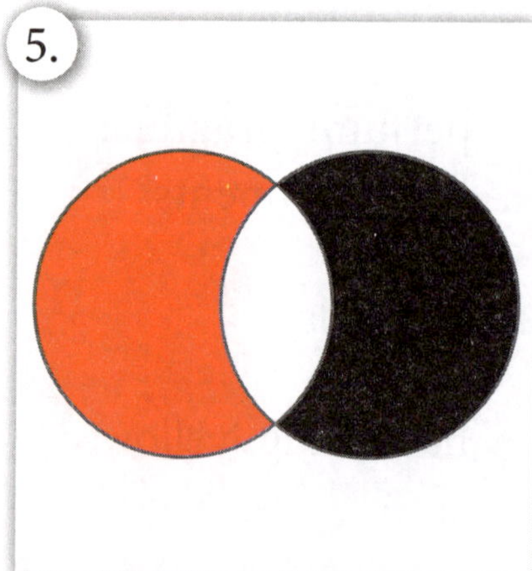

red-black

6.

red-yellow

COOL FACT

If you mix any colour with white, you will get a tint of that colour. If you mix a colour with black, you will get a shade. For example, pink is a tint of red and brown is a shade of red.

B. *To colour these pictures, mix two colours to get a third colour. Now use the new colour, to fill in these picture outlines.*

pigeon

parrot

brinjal

lotus

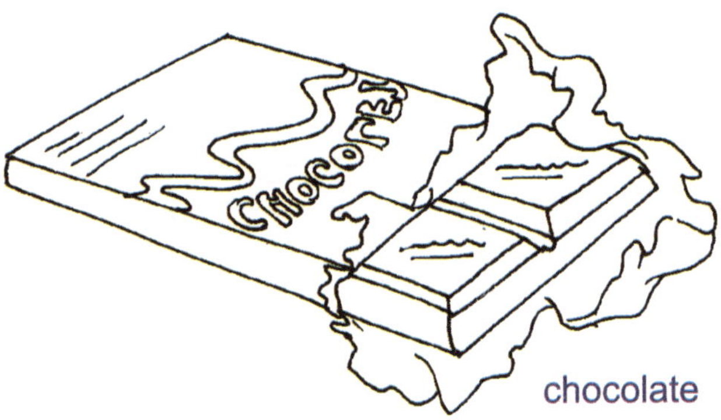

chocolate

marigold

LANGUAGE AND LITERATURE

3

Playing with Letters

What do you do when you have time but nothing to play with? Use words to play games! Try to play these three games.

A. *Use the letters of these long words to make words having two or more letters from each of them to fill in the blanks. One small word from each of the big word has been made for you.*

1.	Beautiful	but	____	____	____	____	____	____	____
2.	Important	pot	____	____	____	____	____	____	____
3.	Refrigerate	fig	____	____	____	____	____	____	____

B. 1. This is a word box. Start with the letter T and make a sentence that makes sense. Each letter can be used only once. You can move either horizontally or vertically, not diagonally.

D	O	O	G
T	E	I	S
H	L	Z	Z
I	S	P	U

2. Now make a word box for this sentence.
You write very well.

C. *This is a six-letter word. Use each of the six clues to guess the letters.*

5. Appears in race and not in each ______
6. Appears in tune and not in true ______
2. Appears in cared but not in crude ______
4. Appears in sure but not in sore ______
1. Appears in sold but not in doll ______
3. Appears in paste and not in space ______

Now rearrange the letters to get the name of the sixth planet from the sun ______________.

COOL FACT

Scrabble®, Jumble® and Crosswords are all word games which often appear in newspapers and magazines.

Score board 3-5 words: Good 5-7 words: Very Good > 7 words: Excellent

AROUND THE WORLD

4

Seasons

People in India experience different seasons.

Read these sentences about seasons in India and write T for True and F for False.

1. We observe Independence Day during the winter season in India. ☐
2. During the winter season, the current year ends and a new year starts. ☐
3. In spring, flowers bloom and new green leaves grow. ☐
4. After spring comes winter, with short days and long nights. ☐
5. In summer, we should wear dark-coloured clothes to keep us cool. ☐
6. In the summer months, the sun makes it difficult for the farmers to work in the fields. ☐
7. Mangoes ripen towards the end of summer and at the beginning of monsoon. ☐
8. During the rainy season, we enjoy the festival of colours called Holi. ☐
9. Republic Day is celebrated in winter in India. ☐
10. Autumn is the harvest season for farmers. ☐

COOL FACT

In many parts of India, the year is divided into six seasons as per the traditional calendar whose Sanskrit / Hindi names are: *Vasant* (Spring), *Grishma* (Summer), *Varsha* (Monsoon), *Sharad* (Autumn), *Hemant* (Pre-winter) and *Shishir* (Winter).

SCIENCE

5 Everything About Fruits

A. *Fruits can be of different kinds. Read the description of fleshy, citrus, dry and mutiple fruits given below. Write the fruits given in the list in different groups.*

Fleshy Fruits have a pulpy wall and seeds in the centre	**Citrus fruits** juicy fruits with a tangy, sweet sour taste	**Dry fruits** hard to bite fruits without pulp	**Multiple fruits** grow from a cluster of flowers

____________	____________	____________	____________
____________	____________	____________	____________
____________	____________	____________	____________

plum	almond	custard apple	jackfruit	walnut	apricot
orange	pistachio	sweet lime	papaya	pineapple	lemon

B. *Read the clues and name the fruits. The help box has all the names in jumbled order.*

1. Grows in bunches and is available all over India ___________
2. The tiny seeds of this small, red-pink fruit are on the outside. _________
3. Grows extensively in the states of Himachal Pradesh and Kashmir ______
4. Grows on a vine and is bought in bunches ___________
5. About the size of a hen's egg, this fruit is hairy brown on the outside and green on the inside. __________
6. The inside of this fruit is full of juicy pink/red seeds. ___________

COOL FACT

Tomato is a fruit, although it is mostly used in cooking as a vegetable.

7. Huge with thorny skin, but the ripe flesh inside is sweet and pulpy _____
8. Huge and green skinned outside, pink or red inside, full of water ______
9. Often used in ice cream, and on top of the icing on a cake __________
10. Oddly-shaped and juicy, found in cold places __________
11. Sweet-sour, used widely in making juice or in cooking __________
12. Known as *peru* or *amrood* from the Persian word for pear __________
13. Called the king of fruits, eaten especially in summer __________
14. Has fuzzy skin, is soft red and yellow, juicy and pulpy inside with a hard seed in the middle __________
15. Fragrant summer fruit, comes in musk, rock and honeydew varieties __________

strawberry	mango	banana	lime	pomegranate	cherry
guava	peach	jackfruit	kiwi	watermelon	pear
apple	melon	grapes			

C. *Find fifteen fruits in the picture below and colour them.*

6 Festivals in India

India is a culturally diverse nation and celebrates many festivals.

Complete this crossword on festivals using the clues.

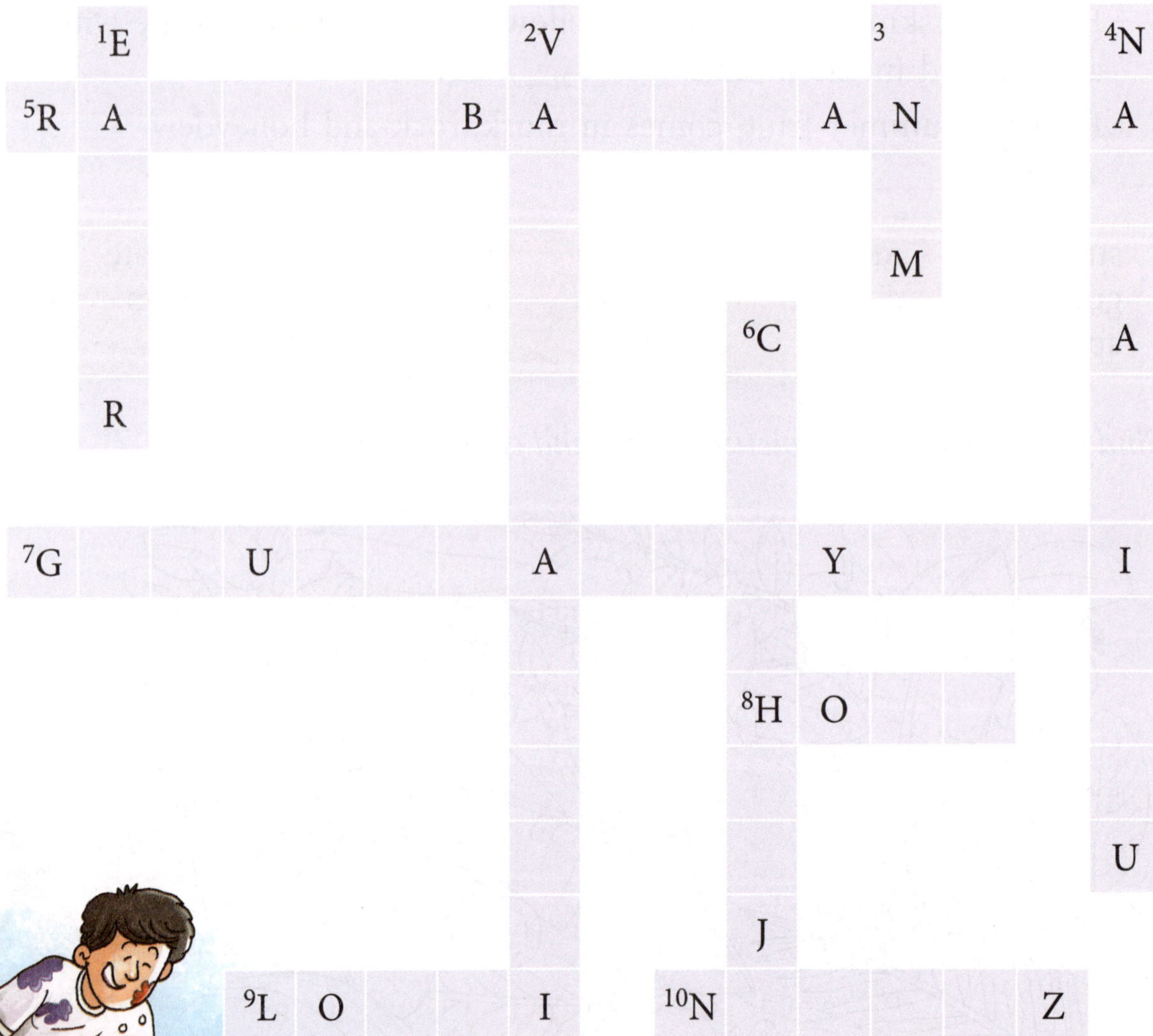

COOL FACT

Dussehra, also known as *Vijayadashmi* or *Bijoya,* is celebrated in different parts of India in different ways. It is celebrated at the end of nine days of festivities.

Clues

Across

5. Celebrated as a festival of brothers and sisters
7. Birth anniversary of the first Sikh Guru, celebrated on the full moon day
8. The demon Holika is burnt in a bonfire and then we all play with colours and water.
9. Celebrated with a bonfire when the sun moves from the southern to the northern hemisphere
10. Celebrated by Parsis on spring equinox to mark the beginning of the Persian New Year

Down

1. Celebrates the return of Jesus Christ from his grave three days after his death
2. Dedicated to the Goddess Saraswati and to the arrival of spring, with the blooming of mustard flowers
3. Celebrates the summer harvest and the homecoming of King Mahabali with a carnival and the famous snake boat race
4. Celebrated over nine nights in South India with dolls and gods displayed on steps
6. Celebrated by offering prayers to the Sun God while standing in the river

7

Animal Habitats and Habits

Complete this crossword about animals, their habitats, their reproductive and feeding habits using the clues.

Clues

Across

2. Plant eating animals
3. Animals that live in water
6. Animals like monkeys, koala bears and sloths that live on trees
8. Animals that live both on land and in water
9. Animals like whales, sharks, star fishes and dolphins that live in the sea
10. Animals that eat both animals and plants

Down

1. Animals like cows, horses, dogs that live on land
4. Flesh eating animals
5. Animals that give birth to young ones
7. Animals like snakes, turtles, sparrows that lay eggs

COOL FACT

Tortoises and turtles are similar but while tortoises live on land, turtles live mostly in water.

SAFETY SCIENCE

8 Reach Home Safe!

A. *You are at school, and the dismissal bell has rung! Take this Safety quiz and make the correct choices so that you get home in the shortest time.*

1. You come out of the class and
   - a. run to your bus and stand just outside the bus door ☐
   - b. reach the bus quickly and stand 3 feet away ☐
2. Why stand 3 feet away from the bus?
   - a. it is outside the "danger zone" ☐
   - b. it is easier to call out to friends from that spot ☐

3. The bus door opens. You climb in
   a. one step at a time, using the handrail ☐
   b. two steps at a time, since there are forty other kids waiting ☐
4. You should climb slowly holding the rail so that
   a. you can look around and choose your favourite seat ☐
   b. you can avoid getting badly hurt ☐
5. On the bus, you sit down and keep you bag and bottle
   a. on your lap ☐
   b. on the seat next to you ☐
   c. in the aisle ☐
6. The bus has left school. Yippee! You pass your time
   a. singing and shrieking, since you are so happy ☐
   b. napping or just sitting quietly ☐
7. Your stop has arrived. You
   a. step off the bus and quickly run across the road (if needed) from the front of the bus ☐
   b. step off the bus and cross the road (if needed) from behind the bus ☐
   c. step off the bus and ask your friend to hand you your bag and bottle ☐
   d. step off the bus and hand your bag and bottle to whoever has come from home to fetch you ☐

Give yourself points for your answers: 6-7 points ☺ 4-5 points 😐 1-3 points ☹

B. *Go over the incorrect choices and discuss with your classmates and teacher why some choices were incorrect. If you chose an incorrect option, what would happen?*

Write down any one here: ______________________________

____

COOL ADVICE

Remember to never loiter in the danger zone of a school bus- which extends 3 metres (or about 10 feet) all around the bus, where children are in the most danger of being hit, either by another vehicle or their own bus.

At a Doctor's Clinic

A. *Look at the picture of a doctor's clinic. Find sixteen things and people shown in the picture using two kinds of clues—anagrams and rhyming words. One has been done for you.*

Anagrams	Rhyming words	Things/people in doctor's clinic
1. suren	purse	nurse
2. crotod	proctor	
3. ocko	book	
4. tapneti	quotient	
5. tontoc	rotten	
6. lurre	cooler	
7. stemich	palmist	
8. blatte	goblet	
9. volges	doves	
10. grinyse	unhinge	
11. cuije	sluice	
12. slepuca	wrap-cool	
13. meintnot	point-vent	
14. slilp	hills	
15. prysu	stirrup	
16. Pil lamb	ship calm	

B. *Four things or people in the list do not belong in a doctor's clinic. Find them and write their names here.*

1. ______________________________

2. ______________________________

3. ______________________________

4. ______________________________

C. *From the picture of the clinic find the following.*

1. two people

   a. ________________ b. ________________

2. two things to consume

   a. ________________ b. ________________

3. two things to apply on the body

   a. ________________ b. ________________

D. *Imagine you had a cold and went to visit the doctor. Write a, b, c... to put the following events that may happen during your visit in the correct order.*

1. The doctor asks you about your cold and your symptoms. ☐
2. Then, he looks into your nose and throat for infection using a torch. ☐
3. You pay his consultation fee and leave. ☐
4. He tells you how to take the medicines and when to come back. ☐
5. He then writes out a prescription for the medicines. ☐
6. Just before you leave, he measures your height using a scale on the wall. He also records your weight. ☐
7. First, the doctor examines your chest, back and the lungs for congestion using a stethoscope. ☐
8. He checks if you also have a fever. ☐

9

The Earth at Our Fingertips

How much do you know about our Earth? Try this quick quiz. The answers are in the help box. But be careful! There are some wrong answers too.

round	red	named	24 hours	fifth	12 months	blanket
blue	life	west	crust	third	dust	covered

1. The outer layer of the Earth's surface is called the ______________.
2. The Earth is known as the ______________ planet.
3. The Earth is the ______________ largest planet in the solar system.
4. The Earth spins from ______________ to east.
5. The Earth is the only known planet so far that has ______________ on it.
6. The Earth is the only planet which is not ______________ after a Roman or Greek God or Goddess.
7. The Earth is not exactly ____________. It is flattened at the north and south poles.
8. The Earth takes ______________ to complete one rotation.
9. The Earth is covered with a _________ of air called the atmosphere.
10. The Earth is the ______________ planet from the sun.

COOL FACT The Earth is the only planet that has one natural satellite called the moon. The moon takes four weeks to revolve once around the earth. Sometimes the moon, earth and sun are in a straight line. This position is called an eclipse.

A Cupboard of Groceries

Mother's grocery list has lots of interesting things to teach us. Apart from fresh fruits and vegetables, here are some foods that you would find in most Indian kitchens.

A. *Match these food types with their descriptions.*

Food type	Description
1. Cereals	a. These are seeds that are a source of cooking oil.
2. Pulses	b. Dried seed, root, bark or other part of a plant mainly used for flavouring, colouring or preserving food.
3. Oilseeds	c. Sometimes called staple foods, they are usually grains. They can be ground into flour.
4. Spices	d. These are dried seeds of plants belonging to the legume family. The fruits are inside pods.

B. *Now sort the foods in the cupboard, on the next page, into the four categories below.*

Cereals	Pulses	Spices	Oilseeds

COOL FACT The rice that we eat is actually the seed of a species of grass.

Balanced Diet

A balanced diet combines food from the three main groups: energy-givers, protective foods and body-builders.

Here is a list of some food items from all the three groups. Each sub-group has a special colour so that you can identify it. Look at these plates. The meals are not balanced. Add two items to each plate.

Energy givers

carbohydrates

roti, potatoes, sugar, rice, pasta, bread

Body builders

animal/plant proteins

egg, fish, chicken, meat, beans, sprouts, lentils like dal

Energy givers

fats

ghee, butter, oil

Protective foods

fruits

strawberry, banana, mangoes, apples, grapes, etc.

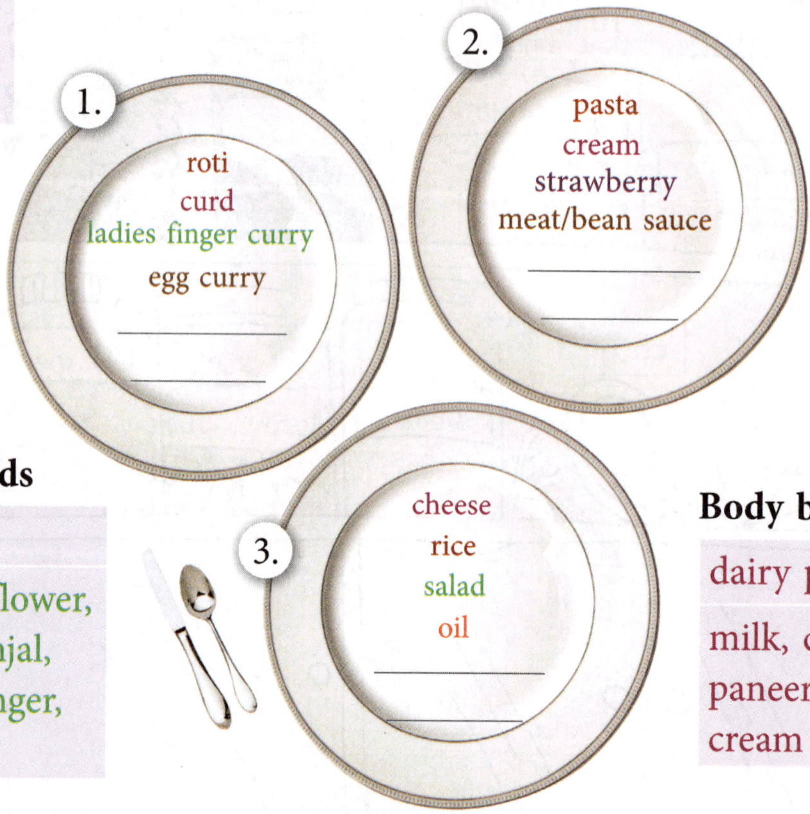

Protective foods

vegetables

spinach, cauliflower, capsicum, brinjal, peas, ladies finger, carrot, etc.

Body builders

dairy products

milk, cheese, paneer, curd, cream

Clue: If the plate has one item from each of the six colours, you know that you have a balanced meal.

COOL FACT Sugar and salt are found naturally in many foods, but we tend to add and eat huge amounts of both, in desserts, pickles and fast food. This is harmful.

0

SCIENCE

What Comes from Where?

Complete the table with a product, the material it is made from and its source. One has been done for you.

coffee bean	idli	woollen jacket	leather bag	peanuts	milk
cotton tree	sap	essential oil	cacao tree	elephant	oyster

Final product	Basic product	Source
1. Tyre	Sap	Rubber tree
2. Chocolate bar	Bean	______
3. ______	Rice	Paddy plantation
4. ______	Animal hide	Goat
5. Coffee	______	Coffee plant
6. Pearl necklace	Pearl	______
7. Groundnut oil	______	Peanut plant
8. Bandage gauze	Cotton balls	______
9. ______	Wool	Sheep
10. Perfume	______	Jasmine flowers
11. Ivory	Tusk	______
12. Cheese	______	Buffalo

COOL FACT

Precious metals are found deep in the Earth inside mines. The deepest mines are gold mines, sometimes more than three kilometres below the Earth's surface.

11 Sports Terms

In this jumble, there are eight common sports and sixteen connected terms, two for each sport. Find the eight sports and the two words that are connected to that sport. One has been done for you.

Boxing			
1. knockout	1.	1.	1.
2. hook	2.	2.	2.

1.	1.	1.	1.
2.	2.	2.	2.

COOL FACT

What do the sporting terms 'raider', 'lona' and 'lobby' have in common? Well, they are all connected with the Indian sport, kabaddi.

2

Sporting Spaces

Every sport is played in a special space that has a specific name. Look at these pictures of sporting places. Match them with the correct sport. Use the help box for the names of these spaces

1.

2.

3.

4.

5.

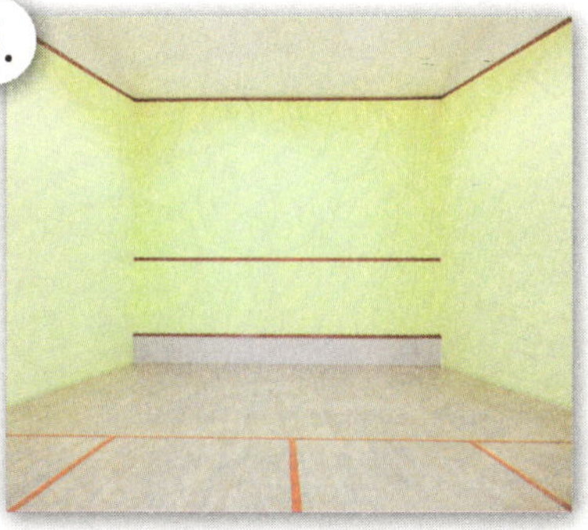

6.

7.

a. football

b. golf

c. skating

d. cycling

e. shooting

f. baseball

g. squash

field	court
range	rink
course	track
diamond	pitch

COOL FACT

The length of a cricket pitch is always 66 feet or 22 yards (1 yard = 3 feet). This is because the pitch was originally measured by a Gunter's chain (used to measure the length and breadth of land), whose total length when stretched out is exactly 66 feet.

LANGUAGE AND LITERATURE

13 The Jungle Book

Identify the animals from this picture. Next to their Jungle Book names, write what kind of animal each one is. (Clue: many of animal names are English translations of their Sanskrit or Hindi words!)

1. Akela – ____________________
2. Raksha – ____________________
3. Bagheera – ____________________
4. Baloo – ____________________
5. Chil – ____________________
6. Darzee – ____________________
7. Hathi – ____________________
8. Kaa – ____________________
9. Mowgli – ____________________
10. Rikki-tikki-tawi – ____________________
11. Shere Khan – ____________________
12. Tabaqui – ____________________

COOL FACT

The jungle in *The Jungle Book* is a real one. It is Pench in Madhya Pradesh, which is a tiger sanctuary, today.

The Number 4

A. *Here are 8 groups of 4 each: The first is filled in, complete the others. The first letter of each is given to you.*

	Fill in the four answers here			
Basic Blood groups	A	B	AB	O
Cardinal directions	N________	E________	W________	S________
Basic math operations	A________	S________	M________	D________
Suits in cards	S________	H________	C________	D________
Houses in Hogwarts	G________	H________	R________	S________
Giant Planets	J________	S________	U________	N________
States of Matter	S________	L________	G________	P________
Strokes in swimming	F________	B________	B________	B________

B. *Answer this short quiz on the number 4.*

1. Of which type of tooth does an adult human being have four?
2. In which sport does the playing arena have 4 bases?
3. Which unit of storage in computers equals 4 bits?
4. People of which religion believe in the 4 Great Truths?

COOL FACT

The Four Corners monument in USA marks the point where the boundaries of 4 states meet at a single point. The states are Colorado, Utah, New Mexico and Arizona

4

Let's Go North

Look at the pictures linked to the five states of India namely Uttar Pradesh, Jammu and Kashmir, Punjab, Himachal Pradesh and Uttarakhand. Two pictures connect to each state. Write the correct letter in the given box to match each picture with its state.

1.

Taj Mahal

2.

Corbett National Park

3.

Golden Temple

4.

phiran dress

5.

phulkari

6.

Kullu cap

a. Uttar Pradesh

b. Jammu and Kashmir

c. Punjab

d. Himachal Pradesh

e. Uttarakhand

COOL FACT

The oldest national park in India is the Corbett National Park. It was established in 1936 and named after Jim Corbett, a well-known hunter of tigers and leopards, especially man-eaters.

7.

shikara

8.

Laxman Jhula

9.
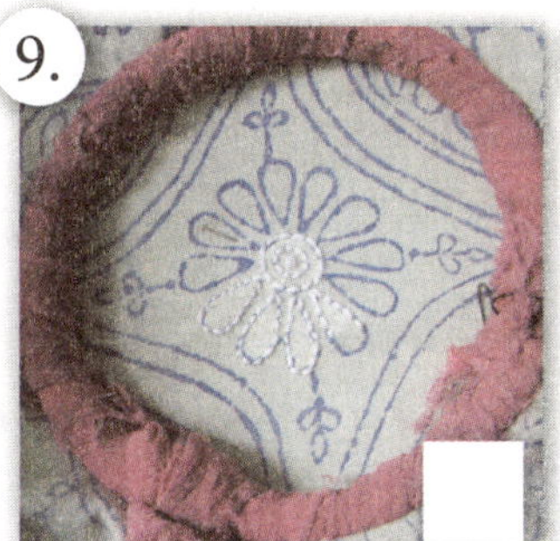
chikan work

10.

Christ Church, Shimla

How to Crack the Indian State Capitals I

HOTS

To learn and remember the names of the capitals of the 29 states of India is not very easy. One way to make this learning fun is to find something special in each fact. By remembering the special fact, which is called trivium (plural: trivia), you can easily recall the fact.

Some trivia about several states and their capitals have been listed below. Which ones do you think you can remember at a pinch?

1. Mumbai—capital of Maharashtra. It was once a cluster of seven islands. These islands, now neighbourhoods in the city, were Bombay, Colaba, Old Woman's Island, Mazgaon, Mahim, Parel and Worli.

2. Srinagar—capital of Jammu & Kashmir (J&K). It is the only Indian state that has separate winter and summer capitals. Jammu is the winter capital and Srinagar is the summer capital. J&K is the only state which has the name of a capital city within its own name.

3. Gandhinagar—capital of Gujarat. It is the only capital whose name contains the name of a person. It is named after the Father of the Nation, Mahatma Gandhi.

4. Chandigarh—capital of Haryana and Punjab. It is the only city in India that is the capital of two states and is also a Union Territory.

5. Patna—capital of Bihar. It is the oldest state capital in India. It is also one of the oldest cities in the world. Once called Pataliputra, it has already celebrated its two thousand five hundredth birthday.

6. Aizawl—capital of Mizoram. It is the only capital and a state that have the letter Z in their names.

8. Thiruvananthapuram—capital of Kerala. It is the longest name of any state capital. We can remember its spelling by breaking it up into 7 parts: Thi-ru-va-nan-tha-pu-ram. Repeat that 7 times and you'll never forget the spelling.

9. Shimla—capital of Himachal Pradesh. The summer capital of British India until independence, it is also a hill town.

7. Kolkata—capital of West Bengal. It was once the capital of India. Its former name was Calcutta.

10. Hyderabad, Jaipur and Bhopal—capitals of Telengana and Andhra Pradesh (until the new capital Amravati is established), Rajasthan and Madhya Pradesh. These were once capitals of princely states in British India.

11. Chennai—capital of Tamil Nadu. It is the oldest town in which the British built a fort and established a city. It grew around Fort St. George. Its former name was Madras.

12. Bengaluru—capital of Karnataka. It is another name for the City of Guards. It is also named after the Kannada word, *Benda Kalu Ooru,* meaning 'the place of boiled beans'.

Trivia Quiz

Play this fun game with a friend or make two teams. Each team has to choose a colour, red or blue and answer questions written in that colour. If you answer correctly, you get 2 points. An incorrect answer makes you lose 1 point, but you still move forward in the game. The team that gets a higher score at the end of the game wins.

1

If you buried a piece of glass, a piece of cotton cloth and an apple in the garden, which one would still be there after a thousand years?

Which of these is the name of a large island—Greenland, Redland or Blueland?

2

You would need a dice to play which of these games—Monopoly, UNO or Scrabble?

Which object will attract rust if kept in contact with water—a gold ring or an iron bangle?

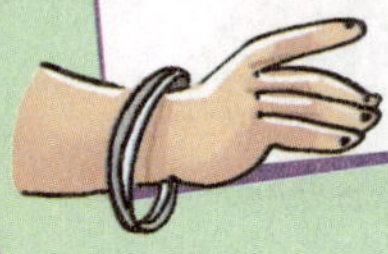

3

Which is longer—a full-size cricket bat or a full-size hockey stick?

Which of these can a cricket umpire signal using only one arm—a four or a six?

4

Which is the highest value currency note printed by the Government of India?

I am a muscle that helps you speak, and is the only muscle which is attached at one end while being free at the other. What am I?

5

A cuckoo bird lays eggs in the nests of other birds. True or false?

Which of these chess pieces cannot move in a straight line on a chess board—queen, rook (elephant), or knight (horse)?

6

What would you use to check your body temperature—a barometer, a thermometer or a spectrometer?

Which of these numbers cannot be written in Roman numerals—0, 5 or 10?

7

Which of these has a 'tail'—a planet, a comet or a star?

In a famous nursery rhyme how many blackbirds were baked in a pie—6, 12 or 24?

8

Which is the largest, a megabyte, a gigabyte or a kilobyte?—

A full-size basketball is smaller than a full-size football. True or false?

9

If your tooth breaks, it will grow back over time and heal itself. True or false?

Where might you see an Eskimo—in the Arctic regions, in the Sahara Desert or in the Brazilian Rainforest?

10

Which of these countries has a flag that appears the same when seen upside down—Japan, USA or India?

Where do most living things live—in the seas and oceans or on land?

11

Which of these fruits has seeds that grow on the outside—strawberries, apples or tomatoes?

What kind of animal was Black Beauty—a dog, a cat or a horse?

12

Which is the only ocean to be named after a country?

Is this true or is this false—in olden times strangers shook hands to show that they were not carrying any weapons?

LANGUAGE
AND LITERATURE

15

A Plural Poem

Read this funny poem on the English language. It is full of singulars and plurals, but not all are correct! Read the clues in the rhyme and fill in the missing words from the box.

We'll begin with box, and the plural is boxes;
But the plural of ox should be 1. ____________, not oxes.
Then one fowl is goose, but two are called 2. ____________,
Yet the plural of moose should never be meese.
You may find a lone mouse or a nest full of mice,
Yet the plural of house is 3. ____________, not hice.
If the plural of 4. ____________ is always called men,
Why shouldn't the plural of pan be called 5. ____________?
The cow in the plural may be cows or kine,
But the plural of vow is 6. ____________, not vine.
I speak of my foot and show you my feet,
If I give you a 7. ____________, would a pair
be called beet?

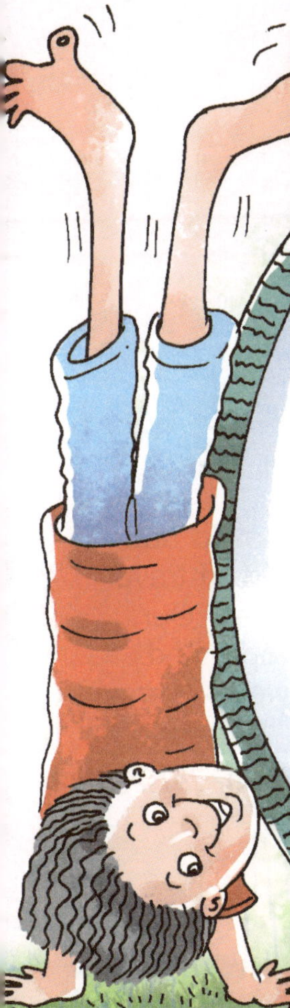

If one is a tooth, and a whole set are teeth,
Why shouldn't the plural of 8. __________ be called beeth?
If the singular is this and the plural is 9. __________,
Why shouldn't the plural of kiss be named kese?
Then one may be that, and three may be those,
Yet the plural of 10. __________ would never be hose;
We speak of a brother, and also of 11. __________,
But though we say mother, we never say methren.
The masculine pronouns are he, his and 12. __________,
But imagine the feminine 13. __________, shis, and shim!
So our English, I think, you all will agree,
Is the craziest language you ever did see.

geese
oxen
vows
man
houses
booth
she
boot
pen
these
him
brethren
hat

COOL FACT Some words in English have no plural form at all. Like staff, furniture, rubbish, baggage, police, etc. Can you think of any others?

My Passport

The word passport comes from two words. The first one is *pass*. The second is *porte* which means 'door'. A passport is a document that helps you 'pass' safely through the 'door' or entry point of a country.

A passport is also a proof of identity, which means it can be shown to prove that you are really you!

> **COOL FACT**
> Citizens of India do not need a passport to travel to some countries. Our neighbours, Nepal and Bhutan, are two of them.

A. *Look at the first page of the passport. Then say if the statements are true or false.*

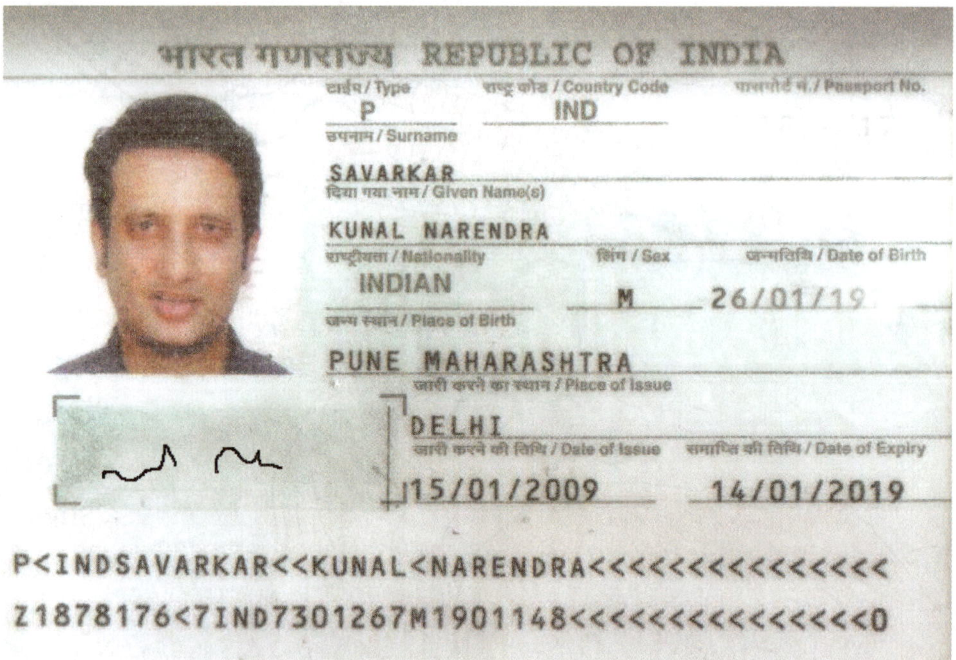
भारत गणराज्य REPUBLIC OF INDIA

टाईप / Type: P
राष्ट्र कोड / Country Code: IND
पासपोर्ट नं. / Passport No.
उपनाम / Surname: SAVARKAR
दिया गया नाम / Given Name(s): KUNAL NARENDRA
राष्ट्रीयता / Nationality: INDIAN
लिंग / Sex: M
जन्मतिथि / Date of Birth: 26/01/19
जन्म स्थान / Place of Birth: PUNE MAHARASHTRA
जारी करने का स्थान / Place of Issue: DELHI
जारी करने की तिथि / Date of Issue: 15/01/2009
समाप्ति की तिथि / Date of Expiry: 14/01/2019

P<INDSAVARKAR<<KUNAL<NARENDRA<<<<<<<<<<<<<<<

Z1878176<7IND7301267M1901148<<<<<<<<<<<<<<<0

1. The name of the passport-holder is written below the surname.
2. The age of the passport-holder is shown on the passport.
3. The details of the passport-holder are written in both English and Hindi.
4. There are three dates written on the first page of the passport.
5. The signature of the passport holder is on his/her photograph.

B. *Match these documents, commonly used as identity cards, with their short descriptions.*

1. This card has a person's photograph on it and it permits one to drive motor vehicles.

2. This is a unique number having 12 digits for each person living in India and has a logo which looks like the rising sun.

3. This card is issued for a family, and allows people to obtain foodgrains, oil and other essential things at low cost.

4. This card is issued by the Election Commission of India to those eligible to vote in elections in India.

5. This is a card with a 10-character code, made up of letters and numbers, issued by the Income Tax Department.

a. Aadhar Card

b. Ration Card

c. Driving License

d. Voter Identification Card

e. PAN

C. *Do you have a school identity card? Write name of your school, draw or stick its logo, paste your passport-sized photograph and fill in other details .*

School logo. ____________________

____

SCHOOL IDENTITY CARD

Session: ________ Roll No: ________

Paste your photograph here.

Name : ____________

Parent's Name: ____________

Date of Birth: ____________

Class: ____________

AROUND THE WORLD

16 

Let's Visit China

China is one of India's neighbours. Like India, it has more than a billion people. Standard Mandarin, the official language of China, is also one of the six official languages of the United Nations.

A. *The Chinese discovered and invented many useful things. Circle four of these seven things for which we should thank the Chinese.*

1. chocolate

2. paper

3. silk

4. coffee

5. noodles

6. tea

7. spectacles

B. *How much do you know about China? Choose the correct options for the questions below.*

1. What are you likely to see at Chinese festivals as decorations and lights?

a. 
Aladdin's lamp

b. 
paper lantern

c. 
diya

2. What do the Chinese use to eat?

a. 
hand

b. 
knife and fork

c. 
chopsticks

3. Which of these is a Chinese symbol?

a. 
dragon

b. 
unicorn

c. 
merlion

4. What is the national animal of China?

a. 
lion

b. 
tiger

c. 
giant panda

COOL FACT

The Chinese calendar associates each year with one out of twelve animals. Some are real animals while others may be mythical. 2017 is the 'Year of the Rooster', 2018 is the 'Year of the Dog' , 2019 is the 'Year of the Pig' and 2020 is 'Year of the Rat'. Find out the others.

LOGICAL REASONING

17 A Visit to the Museum

Look at this picture carefully. Then read the statements. Six of the nine statements are correct. Put a tick (✓) in the box if you agree with the statement.

COOL FACT

Museums can display art, statues, animals, trains and even dolls. In Delhi, there is a museum for toilets.

1. There are more children than adults in this picture.
2. The children's tickets cost ₹100 in all.
3. The cost of tickets for adults is double than that for children.
4. It is Sunday.
5. The museum is about to close.
6. The museum is open from 10:00 a.m. to 3:00 p.m. on Saturday.
7. The dinosaur could fly when it was alive.
8. Photography is allowed in the museum.
9. The man wearing the red T-shirt would have paid ₹270 as entry fee.

NATURAL WORLD

18

Very Indian Animals

India has mountains, forests, deserts, lakes, rivers and the sea of course, so there are many different kinds of animals. Here are some animals found only (or mostly) in India.

A. *Read the line about each animal. Fill in the blank with its name and join it to its picture.*

1. The ________________ is a huge dark grey animal with a horn on its nose. It can be found in Kaziranga, Assam.

2. The ________________ is a handsome animal with a lovely mane. It can be found in the Gir Sanctuary, Gujarat.

3. The ________________ is a mountain animal with beautiful antlers. It can be found in the Dachigam National Park, Jammu & Kashmir.

4. The ________________ is the National Aquatic Animal of India. It is found in the Ganga and Brahmaputra rivers across many states in North and Eastern India.

5. The ________________ is a large grey animal with broad flapping ears and white tusks. Many elephants can be found in the forests around the Nilgiri Mountains in Karnataka, Kerala and Tamil Nadu.

6. The ________________ has a heart-shaped olive green shell. It lives in the ocean and can be found on the beaches of Odisha where it comes to lay eggs.

a. 

Olive Ridley Turtle

b. 

Indian Elephant

c. 

Rhinoceros

d. 

Hangul Stag

e. 

Gangetic Dolphin

f. 

Asiatic Lion

B. *Now, name the animal found in these states.*

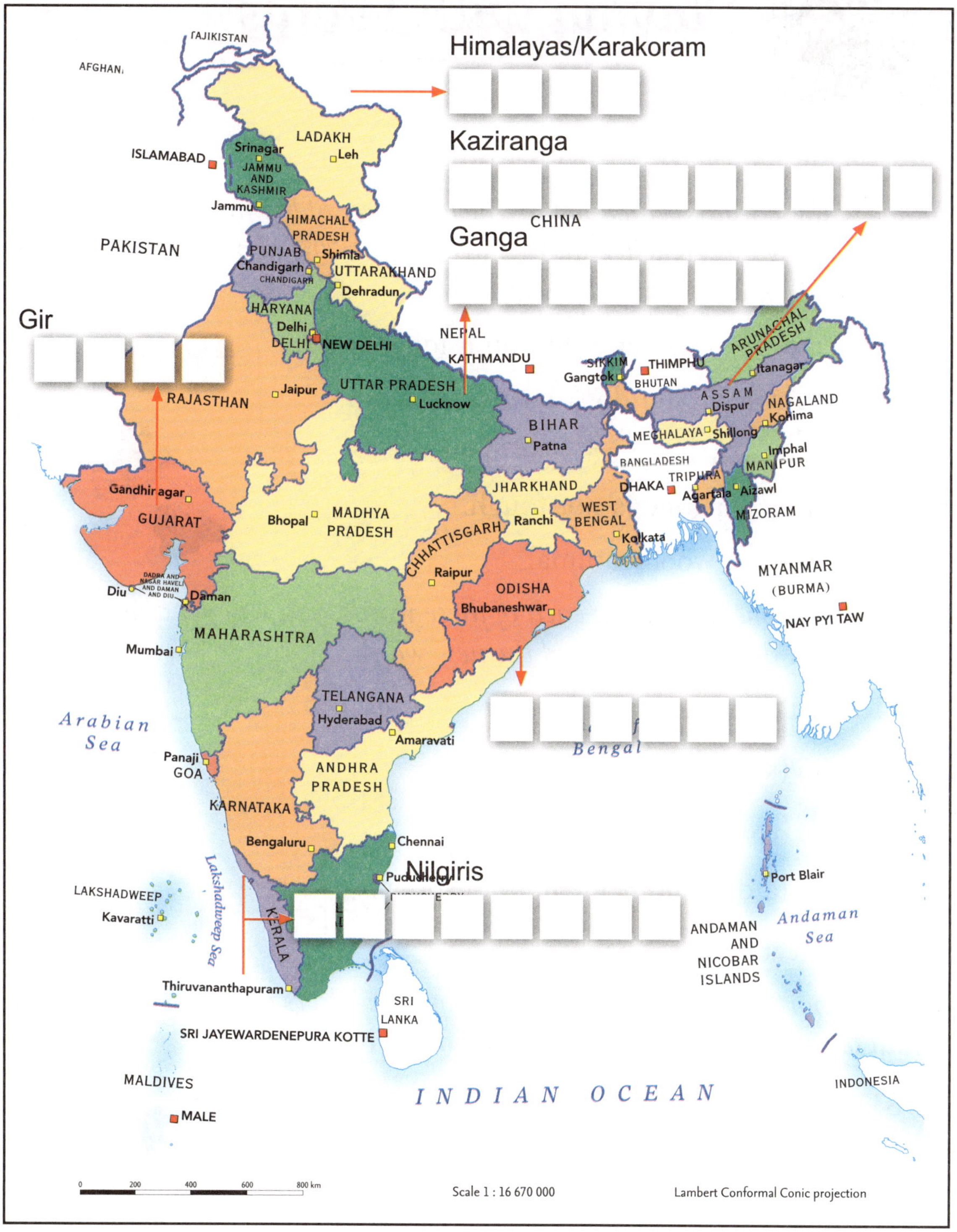

COOL FACT

Most tigers have black and yellow or orange stripes but one kind of Bengal Tiger called the White Tiger, has black and white or almost white stripes. It can be found in the Sunderbans Forests of West Bengal and an area in Madhya Pradesh called Rewa.

LANGUAGE
AND LITERATURE

19

Playing with Words

Play these games and have fun with words!

A. *Complete these words with a letter. The last letter of the first word is the first letter of the second word. To help you, we have given a clue about one of the two words. But the clue is not so straightforward.*

1. Ran(?)ite: Fly this paper toy on a long string. ______________

2. Prou(?)rown: If you don't swim, you will.... ______________

3. Stam(?)ain: Stick me on snail mail. ______________

4. Dat(?)asy: This one is not tough. ______________

5. Shee(?)ray: A woolly animal ______________

B. *If you remove one letter from each of these words, you will get a new word. Use the clues given in the brackets to find the new words.*

1. BRIGHT (one direction) ______________
2. DRINK (skating arena) ______________
3. TRUST (red-brown coating on iron) ______________
4. GRAIN (a downpour in the monsoons) ______________
5. TRIP (tear apart) ______________

C. *All these short words have been made from the letters of the long word written in capital letters, except one. Cross out the odd word.*

1. STATIONERY – stone, section, train, taste
2. EDUCATION – date, diet, team, neat
3. SUPERVISION – person, rope, serve, risen
4. EXAMINATION – nation, mart, team, minute
5. COMPETITION- tempt, item, common, poet

COOL FACT

Pangrams are sentences that contain every letter of the alphabet at least once. The shortest of these, containing 33 letters is:
A quick brown fox jumps over the lazy dog.
Can you make one?

ART

Paper Art

What can you do with a piece of paper? Not much? No, you are wrong, there's plenty you can do!

A. *Look at the names and pictures of some paper arts. Match them with their descriptions.*

1. Collage		a. The art of making different objects by gluing paper strips together.
2. Origami and Kirigami		b. The art of assembling pieces of paper and pasting them, artistically, to form a unified whole.
3. Papier mâché		c. The art of using strips of rolled up paper, shaped and glued together in different designs.
4. Quilling		d. The art of decorating something by gluing coloured paper cutouts onto it, sealed with coats of varnish so that it ends up looking like painting.
5. Découpage		e. The Japanese art of paper folding and paper cutting.

B. *Which of these common objects/articles/things can you make out of paper? Remember, once made, you should be able to use them in real life.*

festoon	kite
envelope	boat
bag	ink-pot
pen-holder	soup bowl
stapler	flag

COOL FACT

Handmade paper is rougher and thicker than normal paper. It can be made from different things, including animal poop.

INDIA

21 Landforms and Water Bodies in India

Complete these sentences about the geography of India. Choose the correct word to fill in the blanks.

1. The fertile flatlands in Northern India that include several river basins are called the Gangetic __ __ __ __ __ __.
2. The very dry area that covers large parts of Rajasthan and some regions of Punjab, Haryana and Gujarat is called the Thar __ __ __ __ __ __.
3. The highest mountain __ __ __ __ in India is K2 or Mount Godwin Austen.
4. The dip between mountains, poetically called the __ __ __ __ __ __ of Flowers, is situated in the Chamoli region of Uttarakhand.
5. The low, swampy land called a __ __ __ __ __, after the fourth letter of the Greek alphabet, is at the mouth of the river Ganga, as it reaches the Bay of Bengal.
6. The Siachen __ __ __ __ __ __ __, in Jammu and Kashmir, is a slow-moving river of ice in the Karakoram Range.
7. The Wular, in Jammu and Kashmir, is the largest fresh water __ __ __ __ in India. It is surrounded by land on all sides.
8. The southern part of India is a __ __ __ __ __ __ __ __ __, which means that it is surrounded by water on three sides. Except along the coast, most of the land here is like a raised table, called the Deccan __ __ __ __ __ __ __.

Desert Glacier Valley delta lake Plateau peninsula Plains peak

COOL FACT

Most rivers in India are named after goddesses. One important exception is the Brahmaputra, which means the 'Son of Brahma' in Sanskrit.

2

Islands

What is common to Sri Lanka, Sicily, Singapore, Bermuda and Mauritius? They are all islands! There are coral islands, volcanic islands, islands in rivers and lakes and even artificial islands! Try these different fun activities about islands.

A. *Choose the correct option.*

An island is:

a. a body of water surrounded by land on all sides

b. a country in Northern Europe

c. a piece of land surrounded by water on all sides

B. *Answer T if True, F if False.*

The largest island in the world is Greenland : T or F?

C. *Read the clue and name the islands. But watch out, there are three incorrect answers in the help box!*

1. Most populated island in the world ☐
2. Largest island in India ☐
3. Most populous island in India ☐
4. Artificial island that houses an airport ☐

a. Great Nicobar (Bay of Bengal)
b. Willingdon Island (Arabian Sea off India)
c. Salsette (Mumbai)
d. Kansai (Osaka Bay)
e. Java (Indonesia)
f. Madagascar (Indian Ocean)
g. Middle Andaman (Bay of Bengal)

COOL FACT

An archipelago is a group of islands. The largest archipelago in the world is Indonesia – with over 13,400 islands!

North Sentinel Island in the Andaman and Nicobar group is home to a tribe of people who have refused to allow any contact, and in fact prevent outsiders from stepping on the island!

23 Birds Galore

Read the clues and complete this bird crossword. One has been done for you.

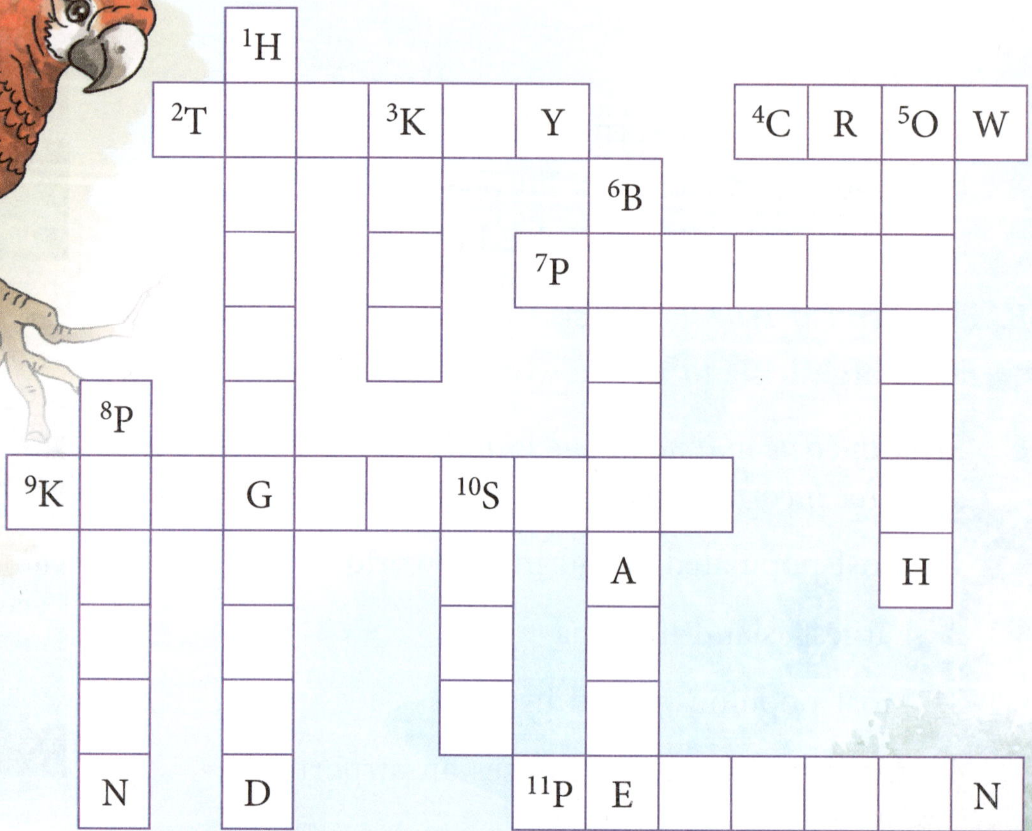

Clues

Across

2. Shares its name with a country, makes a gobbling sound
4. Mostly glossy black in colour, this bird is commonly found in India. A group of these birds is called a murder.
7. Known for its ability to mimic, it makes a wonderful talking pet.
9. As its name suggests, this multi-coloured bird's diet is mainly made up of fish.
11. Found in the Southern Hemisphere, it lives in large colonies, and looks as though it is wearing a formal coat and shirt.

Down

1. Gets its name from the musical sound made by rapid wing beats
3. Found in New Zealand, it shares its name with a hairy-skinned fruit.
5. The largest bird in the world. Found in Africa, it buries its head in the sand if chased by enemies.
6. Although its name suggests that it has no hair, it has a crown of feathers on its head.
8. Related to the dove family, this greyish common bird was trained for carrying messages across long distances in olden times.
10. In a famous fairy tale, this ugly bird becomes very beautiful as it grows up.

COOL FACT The Indian cuckoo lays a single egg in the nest of another bird, usually a crow. So the baby bird is brought up by a foster mother until it is old enough to fly away from the nest.

First Aid

A. *Look at each emergency situation shown below with the three best first aid actions for it. Write the number of the emergency against each action. One has been done for you.*

1.

insect bite

2.

sprain or bone injury

3.

burn

4.
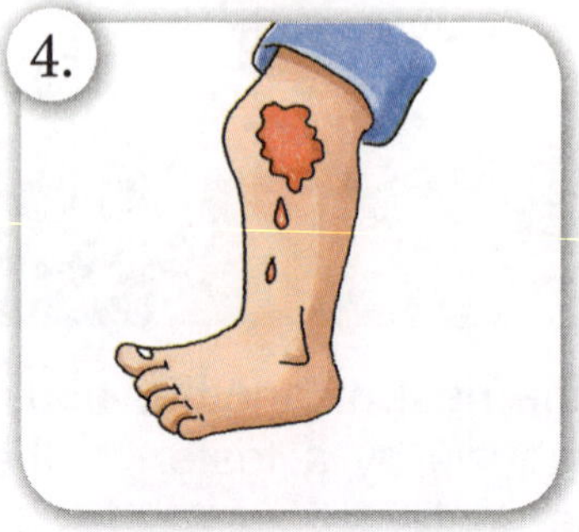
scratch or cut

a. Remove the sting, if any, carefully and wash the area properly with soap and water. ☐

b. Cool the burn with running water till the skin reaches room temperature. ☐

c. Remove jewellery and clothing gently from around the burn. ☐

d. Rest the limb and do not lean on the sprained or broken part. ☐

e. Cover the burn with a sterile bandage or apply a soothing lotion. ☐

f. Apply an ointment or antibiotic cream or powder. ☐

g. Apply a gentle cream to prevent any itching. ☐

h. Clean the wound by rinsing in water thoroughly and then apply an antiseptic. ☐

i. In case of a sprain, apply a cold compress to reduce the swelling and pain. ☐

j. Cover the wound with a bandage to avoid any infection. ☐

k. If the bone is hurt, tie a cloth around it tightly and do not allow the bone to move. ☐

l. Gently dab the swollen area with an ice pack every ten minutes till the swelling goes down. ☐

B. Draw lines to join the emergency situation with pictures showing what can be done.

a.

Gently rinse the eye with warm water. Do not rub or use any solid object like cotton buds to remove the dust or splash water on the eye.

b.

Hold the finger under cold water for the swelling to subside, then apply an ointment or see a doctor.

c.

Rub the area and apply an ice pack.

1. Bruising a leg while playing
2. Bumping the head on a wall/rod
3. Twisting the ankle while climbing up or down
4. Jamming the finger between the door gap
5. Dust falling in the eye

d.

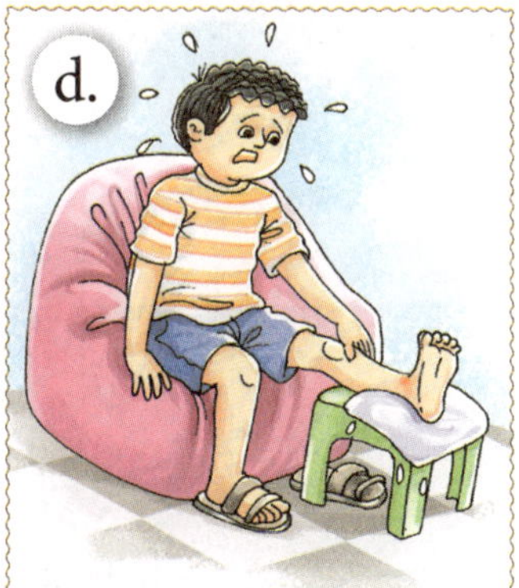

Apply an ice pack so that the swelling is reduced and then wrap a bandage around the area for support.

e.

Clean the bruised area with water and then swab it with antiseptic.

Cool advice: If you get hurt, even slightly, you must tell your parents immediately. Never ever apply or swallow medicines without asking them.

Olympic Cities

The Summer Olympic Games have been played every four years since 1896. Each time the Games are played, it is called an Edition, which is connected with the name of a host city.

A. *Look at these pictures of six very famous cities that have NOT hosted the Olympic Games ever. Identify them and write their names in the spaces.*

B. *Given here are the names of fourteen famous cities around the world that have hosted the Olympics. Search these cities in the word search given below.*

<table>
<tr><td>A</td><td>D</td><td>F</td><td>A</td><td>H</td><td>K</td><td>T</td><td>V</td><td>N</td><td>R</td><td>E</td><td>C</td><td>F</td><td>Y</td><td>U</td><td>F</td><td>D</td><td>Z</td></tr>
<tr><td>U</td><td>T</td><td>Y</td><td>P</td><td>E</td><td>S</td><td>S</td><td>R</td><td>J</td><td>Y</td><td>T</td><td>D</td><td>V</td><td>K</td><td>M</td><td>B</td><td>M</td><td>M</td></tr>
<tr><td>I</td><td>I</td><td>H</td><td>A</td><td>W</td><td>E</td><td>K</td><td>O</td><td>W</td><td>N</td><td>A</td><td>D</td><td>E</td><td>R</td><td>V</td><td>B</td><td>E</td><td>G</td></tr>
<tr><td>E</td><td>X</td><td>C</td><td>R</td><td>Y</td><td>O</td><td>N</td><td>M</td><td>O</td><td>W</td><td>A</td><td>B</td><td>E</td><td>I</td><td>J</td><td>I</td><td>N</td><td>G</td></tr>
<tr><td>B</td><td>F</td><td>G</td><td>I</td><td>X</td><td>U</td><td>B</td><td>E</td><td>E</td><td>U</td><td>C</td><td>A</td><td>S</td><td>Z</td><td>J</td><td>Y</td><td>O</td><td>K</td></tr>
<tr><td>E</td><td>Q</td><td>W</td><td>S</td><td>R</td><td>L</td><td>T</td><td>Y</td><td>U</td><td>D</td><td>I</td><td>R</td><td>P</td><td>O</td><td>O</td><td>R</td><td>T</td><td>W</td></tr>
<tr><td>E</td><td>E</td><td>T</td><td>O</td><td>W</td><td>N</td><td>F</td><td>E</td><td>I</td><td>K</td><td>F</td><td>C</td><td>B</td><td>E</td><td>I</td><td>J</td><td>I</td><td>K</td></tr>
<tr><td>F</td><td>G</td><td>H</td><td>T</td><td>R</td><td>J</td><td>D</td><td>Y</td><td>U</td><td>G</td><td>H</td><td>E</td><td>Y</td><td>R</td><td>G</td><td>S</td><td>F</td><td>R</td></tr>
<tr><td>T</td><td>F</td><td>T</td><td>R</td><td>A</td><td>R</td><td>A</td><td>N</td><td>C</td><td>H</td><td>R</td><td>L</td><td>E</td><td>R</td><td>U</td><td>X</td><td>P</td><td>A</td></tr>
<tr><td>R</td><td>I</td><td>O</td><td>D</td><td>E</td><td>J</td><td>A</td><td>N</td><td>E</td><td>I</td><td>R</td><td>O</td><td>T</td><td>E</td><td>R</td><td>B</td><td>R</td><td>G</td></tr>
<tr><td>D</td><td>A</td><td>K</td><td>H</td><td>V</td><td>R</td><td>I</td><td>Y</td><td>T</td><td>D</td><td>T</td><td>N</td><td>B</td><td>N</td><td>B</td><td>E</td><td>V</td><td>M</td></tr>
<tr><td>W</td><td>Q</td><td>Y</td><td>C</td><td>E</td><td>B</td><td>E</td><td>Y</td><td>R</td><td>S</td><td>D</td><td>A</td><td>S</td><td>E</td><td>G</td><td>R</td><td>U</td><td>O</td></tr>
<tr><td>S</td><td>T</td><td>O</td><td>C</td><td>K</td><td>H</td><td>O</td><td>L</td><td>M</td><td>A</td><td>S</td><td>X</td><td>G</td><td>Y</td><td>I</td><td>L</td><td>P</td><td>O</td></tr>
<tr><td>Y</td><td>R</td><td>T</td><td>D</td><td>V</td><td>N</td><td>R</td><td>E</td><td>O</td><td>A</td><td>N</td><td>P</td><td>U</td><td>T</td><td>E</td><td>I</td><td>N</td><td>M</td></tr>
<tr><td>D</td><td>E</td><td>C</td><td>A</td><td>T</td><td>H</td><td>E</td><td>N</td><td>S</td><td>Y</td><td>L</td><td>O</td><td>N</td><td>D</td><td>O</td><td>N</td><td>K</td><td>K</td></tr>
<tr><td>N</td><td>R</td><td>P</td><td>O</td><td>I</td><td>U</td><td>Y</td><td>T</td><td>C</td><td>R</td><td>E</td><td>W</td><td>Q</td><td>L</td><td>K</td><td>J</td><td>H</td><td>G</td></tr>
<tr><td>E</td><td>F</td><td>D</td><td>S</td><td>A</td><td>M</td><td>N</td><td>L</td><td>O</td><td>S</td><td>A</td><td>N</td><td>G</td><td>E</td><td>L</td><td>E</td><td>S</td><td>B</td></tr>
<tr><td>Y</td><td>V</td><td>C</td><td>X</td><td>Z</td><td>P</td><td>O</td><td>I</td><td>W</td><td>U</td><td>U</td><td>Y</td><td>T</td><td>R</td><td>E</td><td>Q</td><td>Z</td><td>L</td></tr>
</table>

COOL FACT Tokyo first hosted the Summer Olympics in 1964 and will host the 2020 edition as well.

Explorers of the World

Different parts of the world were discovered by great explorers. Look at the routes taken by some explorers in the world map given below and read their descriptions. Choose and write the correct names of the explorers in the blanks.

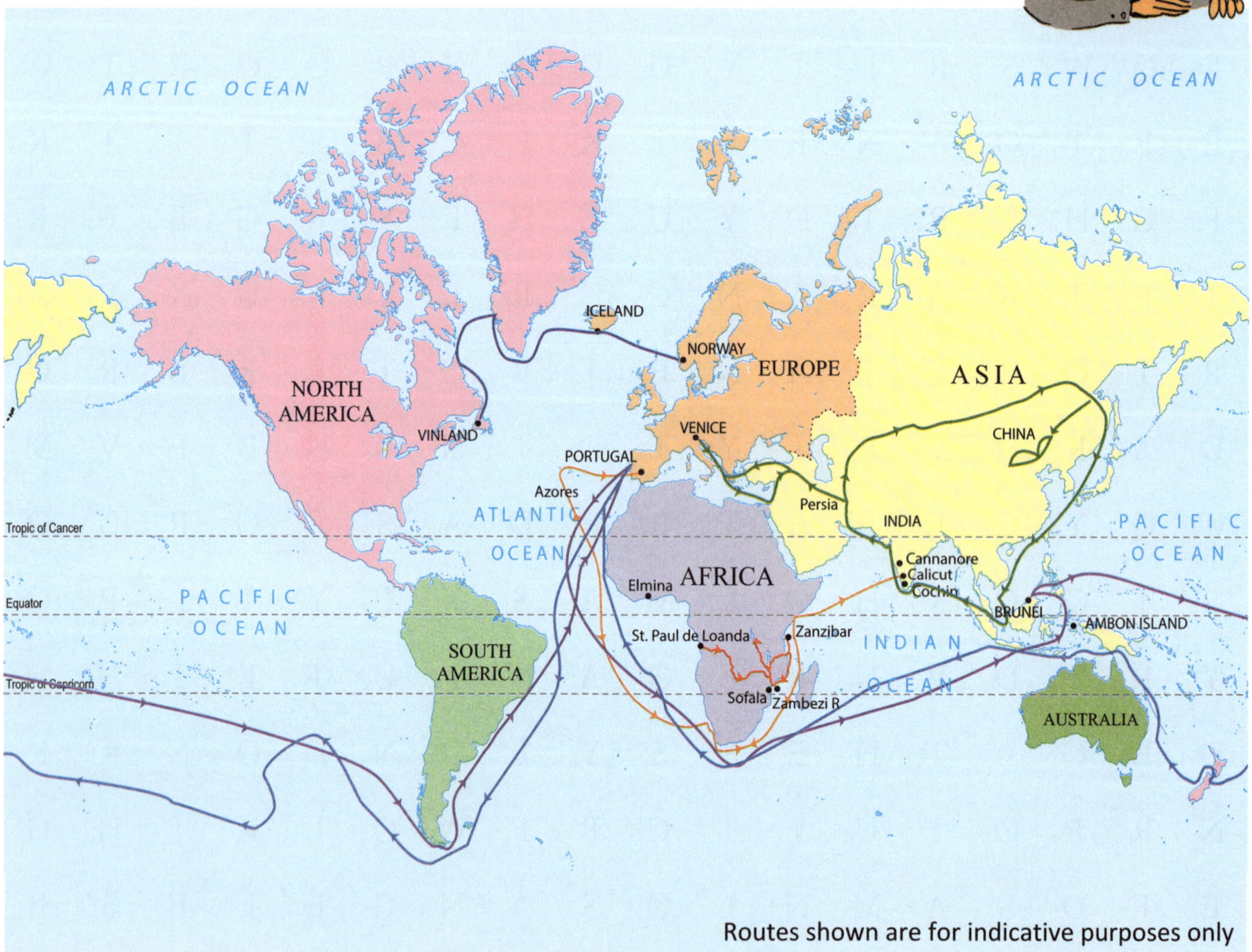

COOL FACT

Although the Vikings were the first to reach North America and Christopher Columbus is credited with discovering America, the name, America, comes from an Italian merchant and mapmaker called Amerigo Vespucci.

1. He discovered the route from Lisbon, Portugal to Calicut (Kozhikode), India.

____

2. He left Norway and visited L'Anse aux Meadows, Newfoundland, North America for the first time about a thousand years ago. ________________

3. He travelled from his hometown Venice, Italy to Dadu (Beijing), China and met Emperor Kublai Khan. ________________________

4. A Portuguese explorer, who set off from Seville, Spain. One of his ships, the Victoria, became the first to sail around the world. It took him almost three years. ______________________

5. An Englishman (England), who explored the South Pacific, Eastern Australia and New Zealand, before he died in the Hawaiian Islands.

____

6. The first European, from Scotland, to see the Victoria Falls on the river Zambezi in Africa.

____

Marco Polo	Vasco da Gama	Leif Erikson
Ferdinand Magellan	David Livingstone	James Cook

COOL FACT

Robert Peary, an American, was the first explorer to reach the North Pole, while Roald Amundsen, a Norwegian, was the first to reach the South Pole.

25

Let's Visit Russia

Russia is the largest country in the world. It spans two continents–Asia and Europe.

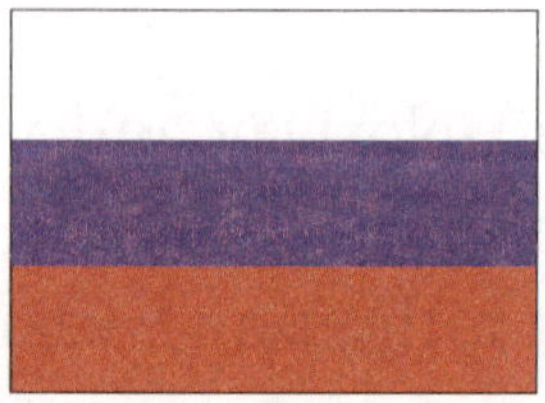

Capital: Moscow
Script: Cyrillic
Currency: Rouble
Language: Russian

A. *Read the sentences about Russia below and fill in the blanks using the words from the help box.*

Troika	time zones	tundra	Trans-Siberian
tsars	Tolstoy	TASS	Tchaikovsky

1. Russia is the largest country in the world and has nine t______________, so when it is morning in one part of the country, it may be evening in another.
2. The Russian kings were known as t______________. They ruled for around 300 years.
3. The Russian novelist, Leo T______________, was the author of famous novels like *Anna Karenina* and *War and Peace.*
4. The T______________ Railway passes through Siberia. It takes eight days to cover the 9289 kilometre distance between Moscow in western Russia and Vladivostok in the far east of the country.
5. T______________ is an important news agency in Russia, similar to the Press Trust of India.
6. The t______________ is a kind of vegetation region across the Russian Plains and in Siberia, mainly consisting of shrubs, grasses, mosses and lichens. This region receives snow for upto 250 days in a year.
7. Pyotr Ilyich T______________ was the composer of the world-famous ballet opera *Swan Lake.*
8. T______________ means a set of three and is also the name of a carriage drawn by three horses.

B. *In this set of questions about Russia, tick the correct answer out of the three options given for them.*

1. The Ob, Yenisey, Lena and Amur are all very long Siberian mountain chains/rivers/railway lines.
2. Lake Baikal/Caspian Sea/Volga River contains one-fifth of the world's surface freshwater.
3. The city of Leningrad is now called Moscow/St. Petersburg/Stalingrad.
4. The Bering Strait is a narrow strip of water, only 85 kilometres wide, that separates Asia from Africa/Europe/North America.
5. The Greenwich Meridian/International Date Line/Arctic Circle passes through the Bering Strait.
6. The first ever animal that went into space was a cat/dog/monkey named Laika.

7. A set of wooden dolls of decreasing sizes, placed one inside another are called Matryoshka/Perestroika/Anoushka dolls.

8. Garry Kasparov/Anatoly Karpov/Vladimir Putin is the name of a President of Russia.
9. The BRIC countries are Britain, Russia, India and China/Bangladesh, Russia, India and China/Brazil, Russia, India and China.
10. Maria Sharapova is a well known Russian gymnast/chess player/tennis player.
11. The city of Sochi, in Russia, located on the Black Sea Coast, hosted the Asian Games/Summer Olympics/Winter Olympics.
12. The world's first artificial satellite was Explorer 1/Sputnik 1/Aryabhatta.

COOL FACT

We think of Russia and America as far away from each other, but Big Diomede Island in Russia and Little Diomede Island in the USA are only 3.8 kilometres apart. See if you can find them on a globe.

INDIA

26 Folk Dances of India

India has a rich collection of folk dances from different states. Here are the names of some states with their dances and their descriptions. Sort them out and write the correct letter and number in the table on the next page. One has been done for you.

Names of states	
1. Assam	2. Punjab
3. Tamil Nadu	4. Gujarat
5. Rajasthan	6. Maharashtra
7. Mizoram	8. West Bengal

Names of dances

a.

bihu

b.

dandia

c.

karagattam or karagam

d.

purulia chhau

e.

ghoomar

f.

cheraw

g.

lavani

h.

bhangra

COOL FACT An unusual folk dance is the *Poikkal Kuthirai* of Tamil Nadu and Kerala. The name *Poikkal Kuthirai* means the 'horse with the false legs'. It has many regional variations: *Saithikoda* in Odisha, *Keelu Gurram* in Andhra Pradesh and *Kachchighodi* in Rajasthan.

Dance descriptions
i. Men and women go around in circles with pairs of wooden sticks, keeping pace with the music.
ii. Young men and women dressed in colourful costumes dance with brisk steps and hand movements.
iii. Vigorous kicks, leaps, and bends of the body set to songs called *boliyan* and the beat of the *dhol*.
iv. Women move round and round wearing swishing skirts, everyone sings together.
v. Women wearing nine-yard saris sing and dance to a fast piece of music and the beats of the *dholak*.
vi. Men tap crossed bamboo sticks open and close while women dance between the bamboo sticks.
vii. A masked dance drama whose themes come from the Ramayana and the Mahabharata.
viii. Ancient dance form performed with water pots and on different surfaces in honour of the rain goddess, Mariamman.

Names of states	Dances	Descriptions
1.	a.	ii.

TRIVIA

27 Flora and Fauna in the North East

North East India is home to some spectacular plants and animals.

Here are some pictures, names, states and descriptions. Tie each animal with its state and description by drawing a line across the sets.

1.

Rhinoceros

2.

Mithun or Gayal

3.

Sangai

4.

Hornbill

5.

Mrs Hume's Pheasant

a. State animal of Assam

b. State animal of Arunachal Pradesh and Nagaland

c. State bird of Manipur and Mizoram

d. State bird of Arunachal Pradesh

e. State animal of Manipur

i. The annual musical festival of Nagaland is named after this bird

ii. Found on the Loktak Lake, in the marshy wetland in Keibul Lamjao

iii. Named after the wife of the founder of Indian National Congress and the Father of Indian Ornithology, Allan Octavian Hume

iv. habitat is Kaziranga national park

v. Scientific name *Bos frontalis*

6.

Red Panda

7.

Clouded Leopard

8.

Orchids

11.

Shiroy Lily

9.

Rhododendron

10.

Phayre's Langur

12.

Nageswara Tree

f. State animal of Sikkim

g. State flowers of Arunachal Pradesh, Meghalaya, Assam, Mizoram

h. State animal of Meghalaya

l. State tree of Tripura

i. State animal of Tripura

j. State flower of Manipur

k. State tree of Sikkim and state flower of Nagaland

vi. It was featured as Master Shifu, the Kung Fu teacher, in the Kung Fu Panda film series.

vii. lady's slipper orchid, foxtail orchid worn by Bihu dancers, and red vanda, the only red orchid in India

viii. Flowers used to make squashes and jams

ix. Since 2008, it is listed as Vulnerable on the IUCN Red List

x. A postal stamp was issued by the Indian Postal Department to commemorate this flower

xii. The wood of this tree is very heavy, hard and strong.

xi. A species called lutung

NATURAL WORLD

28

Which Insect Am I?

How well do you know insects? Here are some statements about common insects. Match their descriptions with their pictures.

1. My name is the same as a very famous international game. Who am I?
2. I am very hard working. You can often see me and my friends wherever sweet food is spilled. Who am I?
3. When I was a larva, I got to eat a special food called 'royal jelly'. My soldiers make a delicious food called honey. Who am I?
4. I live with millions of workers, soldiers, nymphs, king and queens in a colony. I cause serious damage to wood and even buildings by eating into them. Who am I?
5. I am the strongest among the beetles and can pull upto 20 times my weight. The ancient Egyptians worshipped me. Who am I?
6. I have no wings but I can jump upto heights 150 times my own body length. Who am I?
7. I am the heaviest insect and like to live on rotten wood in tropical forests. Who am I?
8. I like to eat only live insects by catching them with my front legs which make me look like I am praying with joined hands. Who am I?

☐ 
flea

☐ 
queen bee

☐ 
cricket

☐ 
ant

☐ 
praying mantis

☐ 
goliath beetle

☐ 
scarab beetle

☐ 
termite

COOL FACT Entomology is the scientific study of insects. The word comes from *Entomos* which means 'insect' and *logia* which means 'study'.

Travelling to a Hill Station

A. *These are some signs you will see when you travel in the hills. Do you know what they mean? Write the meaning of each sign inside the box next to it. Take help from the icons, which will give you the clues. The first one is done for you.*

compulsory ahead or right	men at work	fuel station ahead
narrow road ahead	hairpin bend	falling rocks

B. *Pair up with a friend, use your imagination and draw two signs (or make posters) on:*

1. Do not throw plastic items
2. Do not waste water. It is precious!

C. *What are the important actions and steps that we must take to protect our hills? Think, talk and write about them in your notebook.*

COOL FACT Have you ever tried to say hello, standing on top of a hill, into the valley below, in a loud voice? You will hear the 'hello' being repeated several times and then fading away. This is called an echo.

How to Crack the Indian State Capitals II

You have already learned some interesting facts about state capitals. Here are some cool ways of learning about some more state capitals, so that you never forget them.

1. Bhopal—capital of Madhya Pradesh. According to legend, founded by the famous King Bhoja, it is also called The City of Lakes.

2. Gangtok—capital of Sikkim. It is situated at a height of 1650 meters above sea level. Gangtok means 'hill top'.

3. Itanagar—capital of Arunachal Pradesh. The word *ita* means 'brick' in the Ahom language. The word Itanagar means 'the fort of bricks'.

4. Dehradun—capital of Uttarakhand. It is a combination of two words, *dera*, meaning 'camp', and *dun*, meaning 'low land' or 'valley'.

5. Jaipur—capital of Rajasthan. Also known as The Pink City. It got its name from the pink colour of its famous monuments, Hawa Mahal and Jantar Mantar.

6. Raipur—capital of one of India's youngest states, Chhattisgarh. Chhattisgarh means 36 forts.

7. Bhubaneswar—capital of Odisha. It replaced Cuttack as the capital in 1948. It takes its name from the Lord of the Three Worlds—Tribhuban + Eeshwar—Bhubaneswar.

8. Kohima—capital of Nagaland, one of the easternmost states. Its name means 'the land of the kewhi flower'.

9. Imphal—capital of Manipur. Manipur also means 'the land of gems'.

10. Agartala—capital of Tripura. Agartala is a combination of the name of the tree that gives an oily perfume and a storehouse.

11. Panaji—capital of Goa. Goa is the smallest state in India, on the banks of the Mandovi River.

12. Ranchi—capital of Jharkhand. It is named after the Oraon word for bamboo grove. It was originally Archi, which became Rachi, and is now called Ranchi.

Visit to a Fuel Station

Have you been to a fuel station?

A. *Look at the picture and label the parts. But watch out! There are three incorrect labels.*

diesel pump   air pressure gauge   car wash   mobile phone charging points   bill book   kids' play area   jerry can   fuel station   lubricating oil   petrol pump

COOL FACT

The bicycle is a mode of transport of the common man. It consumes no fuel, it is healthy and cheap–in short, a great combination.

1. ______________________ 2. ______________________

3. ______________________ 4. ______________________

5. ______________________ 6. ______________________

B. *Now choose the correct options to complete the sentences given below.*

1. The main fuels that are sold at a fuel station are ______________.
   a. kerosene and coal ☐
   b. diesel and petrol ☐
   c. diesel and kerosene ☐

2. If a fuel station is 100 m away, this is the road sign you will see ______________.

a. 

b. 

c. 

3. The engine of the vehicle should ideally be ______________ while filling up fuel.
   a. switched off ☐ b. switched on ☐ c. kept idle ☐

4. Fuel stations are ______________ zones.
   a. No Eating ☐ b. No Smoking ☐ c. No Halting ☐

5. The ______________ area is the place found in some fuel stations where the cars are thoroughly cleaned with the help of water jets.
   a. car wash ☐ b. no pollution ☐ c. air service ☐

6. In the air service area, the ______________ are filled with air and the pressure is checked.
   a. fuel tanks ☐ b. exhaust pipes ☐ c. tyres ☐

7. Some fuel stations are authorised by the Government of India to issue ______________ after checking how much black smoke is blown out from the vehicle exhaust.
   a. fines ☐
   b. discount coupons ☐
   c. Pollution Under Control Certificates ☐

INDIA

29 Instruments Used in Carnatic Music

Look at this composition of instruments used in a Carnatic music concert. The names and descriptions of the instruments are given in boxes below. Write the names of instruments against the correct pictures.

a. *Mridangam* - double-sided drum made usually of jackfruit wood

b. *Veena* - stringed instrument found in various forms like Saraswati, Rudra, Mohana and Vichitra

c. *Nadhaswaram* - long double-reed wind instrument with a hard body and a large flaring bell

d. *Kanjira* - small frame drum made of goatskin, belonging to the tambourine family

COOL FACT

Jugalbandi is a unique performance in classical music in which two musicians playing different instruments perform together.

e. *Sruti box* – box providing support in a vocal or an instrumental concert

f. *Tanpura* – a simple stringed instrument used for setting and keeping pitch

g. *Ghatam* – clay pot with a narrow mouth

h. *Violin* – has four strings and is played with a bow

i. *Moorsing* – small harp held between the teeth and played by the hand

Useful Waste

Let's say you had a banana and a plastic toy in your hand. If you peeled and threw a piece of banana into mud, it would be sticky and messy, but after a few days, it would disappear. Disappear? How? It would either be eaten by other creatures or simply broken down into the mud. This means it is biodegradable.

However, if you threw the plastic toy in the mud, it would stay there. Not only for days and weeks, but it would be there for several years. It might be moved away but it would not disappear. This means it is non-biodegradable.

A. *Sort these daily items into biodegradable and non-biodegradable waste.*

dried leaves	batteries	plastic bag	groundnut shells
vegetable peels	gold chain	glass bottle	crushed tissue paper
used bulbs	coconut shell	fruit waste	compact discs

Biodegradable	Non-biodegradable
________________	________________
________________	________________
________________	________________
________________	________________
________________	________________
________________	________________
________________	________________

Food waste can be reused to make rich soil that makes new healthy plants grow.

B. *All you need is a compost pit. Here are the steps to make a compost pit. They are all in a jumble. Write a, b, c... to put the steps and pictures in order.*

1. If you plan to add more scraps, place a wooden board over the pit so that nobody falls into it.
2. Now you can sow seeds in your own underground compost pit and grow a rich garden!
3. Dig the hole for your compost pit.
4. Once you have finished adding the scraps and peels, push in the mud and soil that you had removed in order to fill the pit and cover the compost.
5. Tear up or chop kitchen waste like peels, skins, leaves and stems.
6. Put the chopped waste into the compost pit. Mix dried leaves (rich in carbon) with vegetable scraps (rich in nitrogen).
7. While the compost pit is decomposing, keep it moist by adding water every now and then. The pit will take several months to completely decompose.

SCIENCE

30

Three States

All things can be found in three states: solid, liquid and gas.

A. *In which state are these things found? Write S for solid, L for liquid or G for gas.*

1.  monitor ☐

2.  red paint ☐

3. 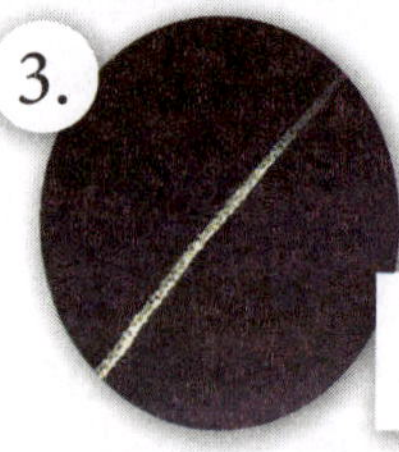 rocket trail ☐

4.  wind from fan ☐

5.  ice cubes ☐

6. 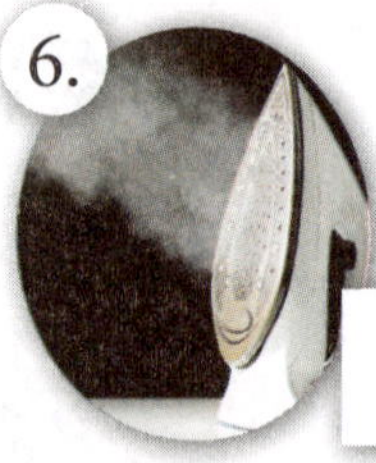 steam ☐

7.  juice ☐

8.  pencil ☐

9.  rain ☐

B. *Solids, liquids and gases have some common and some special properties. Put a tick (✓) in the right columns for each property.*

Properties	Solids	Liquids	Gases
1. have a fixed shape and volume			
2. flow from a higher to a lower level			
3. have no fixed shape			
4. can be squeezed into a small space like a bicycle wheel			
5. take the shape of their container			
6. can always be seen			
7. can flow or spread in all directions			

COOL FACT

Did you know that metals can be liquid too? Thermometers are filled with a shiny and silver liquid metal called mercury.

LANGUAGE AND LITERATURE

Favourite Books

Complete the grid about some well-known stories. The three columns have the name of the work, the name of the author and a short description. Choose the correct answers from the help box.

Name of the story	Author	Description
1. *Alice's Adventures in Wonderland*		A little girl falls into a rabbit hole; meets marvellous and exciting creatures in exotic places and ultimately finds that it was all a dream.
2.	Carlo Collodi	A puppet whose nose grows longer every time he tells a lie; runs away from home and has many adventures. Finally, he becomes a real live boy.
3. *The Ugly Duckling*		Made fun of by his family and friends, a little duckling leaves home and finds that he has grown to become a beautiful swan.
4. *Charlie and the Chocolate Factory*	Roald Dahl	
5.	Rudyard Kipling	A baby boy is brought up by a wolf. Carried by a panther to the human village, he is saved from a tiger who wants to eat him up.
6. *Where the Wild Things Are*	Maurice Sendak	

- A boy goes off in his thoughts to become a Wild Thing, has fun, but then misses his mother and comes back to his room and his hot supper.
- *The Adventures of Pinocchio*
- *The Jungle Book*
- Lewis Carroll
- Hans Christian Andersen
- A boy wins a Golden Ticket to visit the greatest chocolate-maker's factory.

TRIVIA

32

Mobile Telephony

Look at these logos connected to mobiles. Some of these famous companies manufacture mobiles (hardware) and some provide connection and service (software) for the mobiles. Sort the companies into these two groups.

1. 

Samsung

2. 

Airtel

3. 

Nokia

4. 

Sony

5. 

Vodafone

6. 
Apple

7. 

Reliance

8. 

Tata Docomo

9. 

Idea

10. 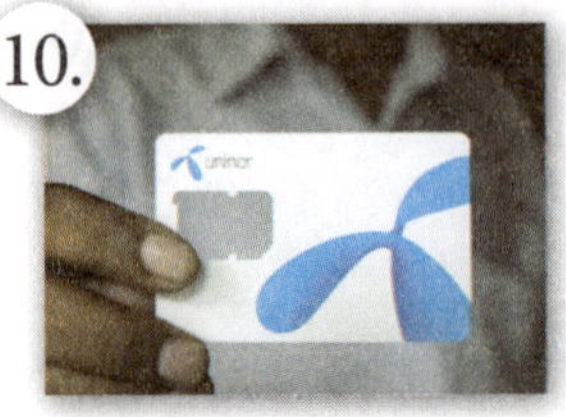
Uninor

11. 

BSNL

12. 

Micromax

13. 

Motorola

14. 

Aircel

15. 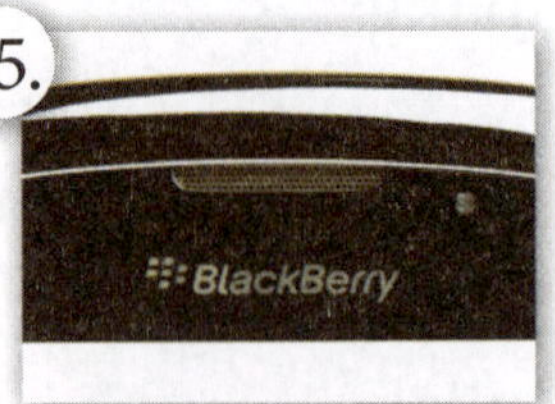

Blackberry

16. 

Redmi

17. 

Gionee

18. 

MTS

COOL FACT

The first call from a mobile phone in India was made in 1995 from Kolkata to Delhi. The mobile network was Modi Telstra, which does not even exist today.

Hardware	Software

B. *Identify these common icons that are found in smartphones. Write their names in the spaces provided. Draw other icons that you know.*

Sporting Spirit

All sports teach us ethics, fair play and the spirit of sportsmanship, which are useful to all of us both on and off the playing field. We should remember and follow these values all through our lives.

Match these sentences about the right way to play a sport and write the correct number-letter combination in the middle column.

First half	Number-letter combination	Second half
1. In cricket, if the ball touches the ground as you have caught it,		a. play the best you can and never give up.
2. In any sport, you should never		b. closest to the opponent's goalpost.
3. In boxing you should never hit an opponent		c. you should not claim a catch.
4. In cricket, if you are on the fielding side,		d. with the umpire or referee.
5. In any sport, if you are playing against a better opponent,		e. you must not make fun of the player who has lost.
6. In any sport, you never argue		f. if he is down.
7. In football, you should pass the ball to your teammate		g. you should not distract the batsman.
8. In any sport, if you win		h. hurt your opponent by unfair means.

Quiz Yourself 1

1. The Indian name for summer is *Grishma* and winter is *Shishir*. True or false?
2. The famous Taj Mahal is located in the state of ____________.
3. We would not need a passport when we travel to Thimpu or Kathmandu. True or false?
4. What is the name given to an animal that gives birth to young ones?
5. The natural satellite of Earth is called the ____________.
6. The Government bans usage of plastic bags that spoil the environment because they are biodegradable/non-biodegradable.
7. What is the national animal of China?
8. Custard apple, pineapple and jackfruit are all single/multiple fruits.
9. Mixing of a colour with white gives a __________ and mixing it with black gives a __________ of that colour.
10. Can you give one other name of the *Vijayadashami* festival?
11. The Central Indian forest on which the book *The Jungle Book* is based is called ____________.
12. In 1995, the first call on a mobile was made in India from __________ to Delhi through the Modi Telstra network.
13. Clove/banana/saffron is a flower used for yellow food colouring and flavouring.
14. Name a liquid metal.
15. The art of using strips of rolled up paper, shaped and glued together in different designs is called __________.
16. Lona, lobby and raider are terms associated with the game of kho-kho/wrestling/kabaddi.

Quiz Yourself 2

1. What is entomology the study of?
2. Pickles have a high content of salt in them. True or false?
3. The length of the cricket pitch is always 22 yards, the length of Gunter's Chain. True or false?
4. Either a Sruti box or a Tanpura is used to provide pitch support in a Carnatic music concert. True or false?
5. The largest fresh water lake of India is the Chilika/Wular/Dal.
6. The name of the ship of the Portuguese explorer Ferdinand Magellan was Lisbon/Victoria/Elizabeth.
7. Elephants are poached mainly for their ____________ as they are very expensive.
8. Paper or cloth bags are used in place of ____________ bags as they are biodegradable and are environment-friendly.
9. What is the name given to foods used mainly for flavouring and colouring?
10. In a famous book by Hans Christian Andersen, the ugly little bird grows into a beautiful ____________.
11. What is the name shared by a New Zealand bird and a fruit?
12. The Summer Olympics are held every 2/4/6 years.
13. The Russian kings were known as ____________.
14. Name the folk dance of Mizoram that uses bamboo sticks between which the dancers move around in rhythm.
15. Which letter of the English alphabet has infinite lines of symmetry?
16. Fuel stations are always No Smoking zones. True or false?

Keys

Page 9: 1. e; 2. g; 3. b; 4. d; 5. a; 6. i; 7. h; 8. c; 9. f

Page 10-11: A. 1. grey; 2. green; 3. violet; 4. pink; 5. brown; 6. orange

2.

E	V	E	T
R	L	L	I
Y	W	E	R
Y	O	U	W

Page 12: B. 1. This puzzle is good C. 5.r, 6.n, 2.a, 4.u, 1.s, 3.t, The sixth planet from the sun is Saturn

Page 13: 1. F; 2. T; 3. T; 4. F; 5. F; 6. T; 7. T; 8. F; 9. T; 10. F

Page 14-15: A. **Fleshy fruits:** plum, apricot, papaya; **Dry fruits:** almond, pistachio, walnut; **Citrus fruits:** orange, lemon, sweet lime; **Multiple fruits:** pineapple, jackfruit, custard apple B. B1. banana 2. strawberry 3. apple 4. grapes 5. kiwi 6. pomegranate 7. jackfruit 8. watermelon 9. cherry 10. pear 11. lime 12.guava 13. mango 14. peach 15. melon

Page 16-17: Across 5. Raksha Bandhan; 7. Guru Nanak Jayanti; 8. Holi; 9. Lohri; 10. Navroz; Down 1. Easter; 2. Vasant Panchami; 3. Onam; 4. Navratri Kolu; 6. Chhath Puja

Page 18-19: Across 2. herbivorous; 3. aquatic; 6. arboreal; 8. amphibian; 9. marine; 10. omnivorous; Down 1. terrestrial; 4. carnivorous; 5. mammals; 7. oviparous

Page 20-21: 1. b; 2. a; 3. a; 4. a; 5. a; 6. b; 7. b;

Page 22-23-24: A. 1. nurse; 2. doctor; 3. cook; 4. patient; 5. cotton; 6. ruler; 7. chemist; 8. tablet; 9. gloves; 10. syringe; 11. juice; 12. capsule; 13. ointment; 14. pills; 15. syrup; 16. lip balm B. 1. cook; 2. ruler; 3. juice; 4. lip balm C. 1. any two out of cook, chemist, nurse, patient, doctor; 2. any two out of juice, tablet, pills, syrup, capsule; 3. lip balm and ointment D. 1. a; 2. d; 3. h; 4. f; 5. e; 6. g; 7. b; 8. c

Page 25: 1. crust; 2. blue; 3. fifth; 4. west; 5. life; 6. named; 7. round; 8. 24 hours; 9. blanket; 10. third

Page 26-27: A. 1. c; 2. d; 3. a; 4. b B. Cereals 2, 7, 10, 14; Pulses 1, 4, 6, 16; Spices 3, 8, 9, 11; Oilseeds 5, 12, 13, 15

Page 28: A. Plate A: one item each from the red and violet lists; Plate B: one item each from the red and green lists; Plate C: one item each from the brown and violet lists

Page 29: 1. sap (given); 2. cacao tree; 3. idli; 4. leather bag; 5. coffee bean; 6. oyster; 7. peanuts; 8. cotton tree; 9. woollen jacket; 10. essential oil; 11. elephant; 12. Milk

Page 30: boxing - knockout, hook (given); hockey - scoop, free hit; lawn tennis - ace, deuce; basketball - free throw, layup; shooting - bullseye, target; golf - bogey, bunker; table tennis - penhold grip, loop; football - tackling, keepie-uppie

Page 31: 1. e (range); 2. d (track); 3. c (rink); 4. f (diamond pitch); 5. g (court); 6. b (course); 7. a (field)

Pages 32-33: 1. he-wolf; 2. she-wolf; 3. panther; 4. bear; 5. kite; 6. tailor bird; 7. elephant; 8. python; 9. human child; 10. mongoose; 11. tiger; 12. Jackal

Page 34: A. 1. A, B, AB, O (given) 2. north, east, west, south 3. addition, subtraction, multiplication, division 4. spades, hearts, clubs, diamonds 5. Gryffindor, Hufflepuff, Ravenclaw, Slytherin 6. Jupiter, Saturn, Uranus, Neptune 7. solid, liquid, gas, plasma 8. Freestyle, breast stroke, back stroke, butterfly stroke B. 1. Canine 2. Baseball 3. Nibble 4. Buddhism

Page 35: 1. a; 2. e; 3. c; 4. b; 5. c; 6. d; 7. b; 8. e; 9. a; 10. d

Page 38-39: Blue set: 1. Greenland; 2. Monopoly; 3. Four; 4. Two Thousand rupees; 5. Knight; 6. Thermometer; 7. 24; 8. Gigabyte; 9. Arctic regions; 10. Japan; 11. Horse; 12. Indian

Red Set: 1. A piece of glass 2. An iron bangle 3. Hockey stick 4. Tongue 5. True 6. 0 7. Comet 8. False 9. False 10. In the seas and oceans 11. Strawberries 12. True

Page 40-41: 1. oxen; 2. geese; 3. houses; 4. man; 5. pen; 6. vows; 7. boot; 8. booth; 9. these; 10. hat; 11. brethren; 12. him; 13. She

Page 42-43: A. 1. True; 2. False; 3. False; 4. True; 5. False B. 1. c; 2. a; 3. b; 4. d; 5. e

Page 44-45: A. paper, silk, noodles and tea B. 1. b; 2. c; 3. a; 4. c

Page 46-47: 1, 3, 5, 7, 8, 9

Page 48-49: A. 1. c; 2. f; 3. d; 4. e; 5. b; 6. a; B. Jammu & Kashmir: Hangul Stag; Assam: Rhinoceros; Gujarat: Lion; Uttar Pradesh: Dolphin; Odisha: Turtle; Nilgiris: Elephant

Page 50: A. 1. k; 2. d; 3. p; 4. e; 5. p B. 1. right; 2. rink; 3. rust; 4. rain; 5. rip C. 1. section; 2. team; 3. serve; 4. mart; 5. common

Page 51: A. 1. b; 2. e; 3. a; 4. c; 5. d B. festoons, envelope, bag, pen holder, lanterns, kites, boats, flag

Page 52: 1. Plains; 2. Desert; 3. peak; 4. Valley; 5. delta; 6. Glacier; 7. lake; 8. peninsula, Plateau

Page 53: A. c B. True; C. 1. e. Java (Indonesia); 2. g. Middle Andaman (Bay of Bengal); 3. c. Salsette (Mumbai); 4. d. Kansai (Osaka Bay)

Page 54-55: Across 2. turkey; 4. crow (given); 7. parrot; 9. kingfi sher; 11. penguin; Down 1. hummingbird; 3. kiwi; 5. ostrich; 6. bald eagle; 8. pigeon; 10. swan

Page 56-57: A. 1. a, f, l; 2. d, i, k; 3. b, c, e; 4. g, h, j B. 1. e; 2. c; 3. d; 4. b; 5. A

Page 58-59: A. 1. Cape Town; 2. Cairo; 3. Bangkok; 4. New York; 5. New Delhi; 6. Dubai
B.

A	D	F	A	H	K	T	V	N	R	E	C	F	Y	U	F	D	Z
U	T	Y	P	E	S	S	R	J	Y	T	D	V	K	M	B	M	M
I	I	H	A	W	E	K	O	W	N	A	D	E	R	V	B	E	G
E	X	C	R	Y	O	N	M	O	W	A	B	E	I	J	I	N	G
B	F	G	I	X	U	B	E	E	U	C	A	S	Z	J	Y	O	K
E	Q	W	S	R	L	T	Y	U	D	I	R	P	O	O	R	T	W
E	E	T	O	W	N	F	E	I	K	F	C	B	E	I	J	I	K
F	G	H	T	R	J	D	Y	U	G	H	E	Y	R	G	S	F	R
T	F	T	R	A	R	A	N	C	H	R	L	E	R	U	X	P	A
R	I	O	D	E	J	A	N	E	I	R	O	T	E	R	B	R	G
D	A	K	H	V	R	I	Y	T	D	T	N	B	N	B	E	V	M
W	Q	Y	C	E	B	E	Y	R	S	D	A	S	E	G	R	U	O
S	T	O	C	K	H	O	L	M	A	S	X	G	Y	I	L	P	O
Y	R	T	D	V	N	R	E	O	A	N	P	U	T	E	I	N	M
D	E	C	A	T	H	E	N	S	Y	L	O	N	D	O	N	K	K
N	R	P	O	I	U	Y	T	C	R	E	W	Q	L	K	J	H	G
E	F	D	S	A	M	N	L	O	S	A	N	G	E	L	E	S	B
Y	V	C	X	Z	P	O	I	W	U	U	Y	T	R	E	Q	Z	L

Page 60-61: 1. Vasco da Gama; 2. Leif Erikson; 3. Marco Polo; 4. Ferdinand Magellan; 5. James Cook; 6. David Livingstone

Page 62-63: A. 1. time zones; 2. tsars; 3. Tolstoy; 4. Trans-siberian; 5. TASS; 6. tundra; 7. Tchaikovsky; 8. troika B. 1. rivers; 2. Lake Baikal; 3. St. Petersburg; 4. North America; 5. International Date Line; 6. dog; 7. Matryoshka; 8. Vladimir Putin; 9. Brazil, Russia, India and China; 10. tennis player; 11. Winter Olympics; 12. Sputnik 1

Page 64-65: 1. a, ii; 2. h, iii; 3. c, viii; 4. b, i; 5. e iv; 6. g, v; 7. f, vi; 8. d, vii

Page 66-67: 1. a. iv; 2. b. v; 3. e. ii; 4. d. i; 5. c. iii; 6. f. vi; 7. h. ix; 8. g. vii; 9. k. viii; 10. i. xi; 11. j. x; 12. l. xii

Page 68: 1. cricket; 2. ant; 3. queen bee; 4. termite; 5. scarab beetle; 6. flea; 7. goliath beetle; 8. praying mantis

Page 69: 1. falling rocks (given); 2. compulsory ahead or right; 3. hairpin bend; 4. petrol pump ahead; 5. narrow road ahead; 6. men at work

Page 72-73: A. 1. diesel pump; 2. petrol pump; 3. lubricating oil; 4. car wash; 5. air pressure gauge; 6. jerrycan B. 1. b; 2. b; 3. a; 4. b; 5. a; 6. c; 7. a

Page 74-75: 1. sruti box; 2. moorsing; 3. kanjira; 4. nadhaswaram; 5. veena; 6. tanpura; 7. violin; 8. mridangam; 9. ghatam

Page 76-77: A. Biodegradable vegetable peels, groundnut shells, dried leaves, crushed tissue paper, coconut shell, fruit waste; Non-Biodegradable glass bottle, batteries, plastic bag, gold chain, compact discs, used bulbs B. 1. e; 2. g; 3. b; 4. d; 5. a; 6. c; 7. f

Page 78: A. 1. S; 2. L; 3. G; 4. G; 5. S; 6. G; 7. L; 8. S; 9. L B. 1. solids; 2. liquids; 3. liquids, gases; 4. liquids, gases; 5. liquids, gases; 6. solids, liquids; 7. liquids, gases

Page 79: 1. Lewis Carroll; 2. The Adventures of Pinocchio; 3. Hans Christian Anderson; 4. A boy wins a Golden Ticket to visit the greatest chocolate-maker's factory; 5. The Jungle Book; 6. A boy goes off in his thoughts to become a Wild Thing, has fun, but then misses his mother and comes back to his room and his hot supper.

Page 80-81: A. Hardware Samsung, Nokia, Sony, Apple, Micromax, Motorola, Blackberry, Redmi, Gionee Soft ware Airtel, Vodafone, Reliance, Tata Docomo, Idea, Uninor, BSNL, Aircel, MTS B. Google Maps, Skype, WhatsApp, Viber, YouTube, Google, Translate, Google Earth

Page 82: 1. c; 2. h; 3. f; 4. g; 5. a; 6. d; 7. b; 8. e

Page 83: 1. True; 2. Uttar Pradesh; 3.True; 4. Mammal; 5. Moon; 6. Non-biodegradable; 7. Asia; 8. Multiple Fruits; 9. Tint, Shade; 10. Bijoya; 11. Pench; 12. Kolkata; 13. Saffron; 14. Mercury; 15. Quilling; 16. Kabaddi

Page 84: 1. Insects; 2. True; 3. True; 4. True; 5. Wular; 6. Victoria; 7. Giant Panda; 8. Plastics; 9. Spices; 10. Swan; 11.Kiwi; 12. 4; 13. Tsars; 14. Cheraw; 15. O; 16. True